Shadows of Love

Bonnie Pike

Illustrator/Photographer/Cover
T. L. Fernow

AuthorHouse™
1663 Liberty Drive
Bloomington, IN 47403
www.authorhouse.com
Phone: 1-800-839-8640

© 2011 Bonnie Pike. All rights reserved.

No part of this book may be reproduced, stored in a retrieval system, or transmitted by any means without the written permission of the author.

First published by AuthorHouse   1/31/2011

ISBN: 978-1-4567-3124-3 (sc)
ISBN: 978-1-4567-3123-6 (hc)
ISBN: 978-1-4567-3122-9 (e)

Library of Congress Control Number: 2011901800

Printed in the United States of America

Any people depicted in stock imagery provided by Thinkstock are models, and such images are being used for illustrative purposes only.
Certain stock imagery © Thinkstock.

This book is printed on acid-free paper.

Because of the dynamic nature of the Internet, any Web addresses or links contained in this book may have changed since publication and may no longer be valid. The views expressed in this work are solely those of the author and do not necessarily reflect the views of the publisher, and the publisher hereby disclaims any responsibility for them.

DEDICATED TO:

Tom:
A truly dominant star (drawing others to him),
a warrior, a patriot,
and a gentle gift of light and hope.
My reason, my purpose, my life.

And to my granddaughter
Jessica:
my rainbow, my sunshine
my treasure
… whom I love more than life itself.

Thank you both for letting me love you
Even for so short a time.

You gave me reason.

ABOUT THE AUTHOR

Written by Gary Lemcke

Where does someone find inspiration? If you ask a roomful of writers where they get theirs, you will probably get a room full of answers; all of them totally different from the next:

For some, it can come in the form of a loved one; the one you picked up and held in your arms when they were born, or the one you held as they breathed their last breath.

For some, it can be found in a walk on a brisk N.Y. autumn day sharing the sun with crimson colored leaves.

For some, it can even be found in the smell of hot coffee brewing on a morning after...

Some can find that inspiration in a dog's friendly bark or the laughter of a child.

Still others, like me, can find it in a lifelong friend's experience that was shared with you and allowed you to feel every emotion right along with them.

Inspiration can from:
 A dream
 A tragedy
 A disease
 Or that illness that everyone feels at some time in their life but which the world's best doctors and surgeons can't put their hands on it to heal; heartache.

Within the confines of the cover of this book, you will find a writer who has found her inspiration in all of these things and managed to take all of these special moments, place them in poetic form, and allow the reader to feel in their own right all of the things that consist of what we humans call life.

Bonnie Pike was born on June 8, 1956 in the small town of Westfield N.Y. to Janice Bemis Gernatt and George Tresler. At the age of 2 and a half, she was placed into the foster care system and later adopted by Edward and Mary Breuilly when she was four and a half years old. The small town of Albion N.Y. became her hometown. Fourteen years later, she married her high school sweetheart on August 10, 1974 and immediately became a Navy wife.

Bonnie and Doug produced three wonderful children and, since 1998, she has been blessed with the addition of six grandchildren. A Navy career man from 1972-1992, Doug became terminally ill in 1997 and passed away in 1998, proving once again that life is indeed far too short.

Throughout her life, Bonnie has given the enduring hand of support for those people among us that we tend to ignore as we pass through the pinnacles and pitfalls of our own lives. Bonnie knew all too well, having been a recipient of the dark shadows of child abuse, that every human being is worthy of love and support in some fashion. Her love for children is always evident. While living in Pensacola Florida, she established the first Cub Scout Pack for emotionally and mentally challenged boys; Pack 645 sponsored by the Al Gray chapter of the Disabled American Vets. She also worked with the Campfire Kids and 4-H programs. Then, as the panic of AIDS continued to grow, she became a volunteer in support programs for the victims and their families. She gave the gift of love, touch, and support to dying men when most of the world turned away from them.

Writing poetry comes as naturally to Bonnie as taking a breath of the first air of the day is to the rest of us. She was first published in 1972, writing a collection of works entitled "A Teenager's Thoughts on Life." While living in Pensacola, Bonnie also became an active member of the West Florida Literary Federation where she participated in the Back Door Poets monthly poetry readings, produced and directed the Reader's Showcase and served for a year on the Board of Directors. She has been featured in the "Emerald Coast Review," "The Poet's Voice," "Amelia," the Back Door Poets chapbook, the Panhandler, and "Home Life."

In October of 2002, Bonnie published her first solo book of poetry which is titled "Survive the Shadow Stalker: A Poetic Journey through Abuse." The poems that grace the pages of this book detail not only the personal survival of abuse, but of the tragedy of abuse suffered from the blind hand of illness, rape, war, and loneliness.

Bonnie possesses the unique gift of being able to put down on paper a feeling or thought that every one of us might have had at one time in our lives. She will not only touch your heart with the poetry that flows from her, but she will have you pull it out and touch it as well; to feel it's warmth; to feel it's aches. She will touch the deepest part of your soul.

PRELUDE

Once, only a short while ago, I honestly did not believe in fate. I felt certain that everything that happened to us was determined totally by our own actions; that we were truly the captains of our own destiny. Then, I was involved in an amazing train wreck (allegorically speaking) that taught me quite quickly how very wrong I have been for all these years.

Although I have known love in so many forms, and given all I have to give in return over my 54 years of life, it was not until quite recently that I learned I had never been **in** love. Oh, please do not misunderstand me, I was married for over 23 years to a wonderful man, and I have no regrets. Yes, I did love him, honored him, served him, and together we had three wonderful children. After his death, despite the fact that I continued to reach out to everyone, loved my family, and yes, even dated, I basically pulled the blinds to my life and feelings closed tight and allowed not one shred of light to come in. Then, unexpectedly, and believe me **NOT** intentionally, I met the man who would and did change my entire world and even some of my long held belief systems. What had always been a world of grays, suddenly become filled with every color of the spectrum, as this man introduced me to feelings I had never allowed myself to feel; and renewed old ones now long held dormant. Due to years of abuse, to believing that I was not entitled to those feelings, and to a belief that I was placed here only to serve others, I had never allowed myself to feel anything but useful (or used). In the space of less the six years, this changed dramatically. Where I still feel the strong need to serve and to be useful, I am also more aware of the need to be the very best that I can be in order to be able to love fully and care for others completely.

I finally learned to appreciate almost every love song I had ever heard. I really learned the meaning behind the Beatles lyrics of: "though I know I will never lose affection, for people and things that went before… in my life I have loved you more…". I learned that it was okay to love someone so much it hurts. I learned what it meant to want to give every part of myself to one person, even if it meant I would have nothing left to give to anyone else ever again. Then, I learned what it meant to lose the thing most precious to you… your heart.

Some of the poems contained within these covers were contained in an earlier book I wrote entitled "Survive the Shadow Stalker; A Poetic Journey through Abuse." Along with the reality of the love, the surrender, and the hope I now have for this man who taught me so much in the later years of my life, this book also deals with the love of: a widow for her long dead spouse, of friendship between men and this woman (with Gary Lemke, Brian Durham, Charles P., William Wilkins, Tom McCloud, Don Bradshaw, Dr. Jack Brooking, Bob Mizer, Gerald Garrett, and James(Bubba) Bosworth, of the love within a family (my children; Mary, Douglas, and James, and my grandchildren: Jessica, James C., Zavier, Shy, Ksondra, Shane, and Crystal), special friendships shared only by women, and, in some cases the most important type of love, the love of self.

This lonely woman, who has always had to play in the shadows, and who only recently felt the real warmth of a bright star on her face, offers this book to you with love and joy. May it be a reminder to all who open its pages of what the power of love can and will do when you are opened fully to receive it and give it.

May it be a living memory to the man who showed me the way of real love and who forever will hold my heart in his strong hands. May it also be a legacy to my children, my grandchildren, to my friends, and to my first love, Douglas J Pike.

YOU ARE LOVED!

SHADOWS OF LOVE

Salt water stained and smudged,
This shattered child of the sun has turned to shadow.
Deep in the wells of her crystal heart
Lies pain.
Confusion.
And fear.

This child of light has lost her way
Along the scattered, broken paths that each new challenge brings.
Pleading eyes beg to go back to the place that once was,
But such a place never really existed; not for her.
Alone,
This child of the shadows now stumbles as her screams go unheard.

Death,
Its job being accomplished,
Lies its head back onto its pillow
And gently eases her into a dream
A dream of
Love…

Follow me…
Follow me now
In the dance of shadow play…

Follow me
In the dance of love...

I BEGIN AGAIN.

What should I to do
with this rambling piece of prosody,
Spenser-like epic of small details,
connected by gossamer threads
of memory--

Flashbacks of laughter and love
Of nurturing and sacrifice
Of making love and being loved

Nightmares of empty places,
empty words,
empty, angry, hurtful, people?
Fear of the great "nothing"?

The ideas of life just wander
'til' another stanza ends,
and I set my pen aside
until I must pick it up again,

And then
Even highlighted,
I cannot find my place.
I begin again.

THE ATTIC OF MY MIND

Sepia drenched memories
Scented with German ice wine
Fade into a collage of clutter
In the attic of my mind

Accidental acquisitions
Piled on forsaken treasures
Tarnished by attainment
Accumulating kindred dust

Wispy tendrils of lavender innocence
Like sachets amidst moth-strewn rags
Garments of disguise and deceit
Worn when darkness whispered seduction

Mottled grape grudges shrunken into bitter raisins
Lay scattered on the floor
Amidst shimmering pearls of forgiveness
Too few and far between

Jumbled puzzles of disjointed words
Some yet to be opened and spoken aloud
Tender gifts given with gentle caresses
Nestle, now, with spiky gauntlets thrown in anger

Embedded images adorn pseudo-walls
Ghostly portraits of friends and family
Some proven no longer so
Maybe never were

Speaking their dialogue in conjured voices
Playing to the script of my memory
Screaming in voices of reality

Pieces of an ephemeral puzzle
Too chaotic to be solved in my lifetime
Gilded treasure clutter increasing exponentially
With the passing of every leaden second

Shadows of Love

From the whispering hills
ancient spirits cry
as a lone wolf sings sadly

the creek is quiet
though it flows underground
the banks vacant and dry
Like my soul

faces carved in stone
the hawk fears not
other nocturnal fare
feel the same

tears fall in silence
but so heavily on the soul
from a heart's greatest pain

my need is like a fever
that searches for unconditional love
but there is only the echo of my sighs

shadows cover the moon
and stars
as my heart now
slowly dies.

DON'T BE AFRAID TO LOVE ME

I lived for those nights when you fell asleep next to me
and I listened to your breathing soften and deepen
as you drifted off in dreams.
I imagined myself whispering to you as you slept.
Telling you not to be afraid of this,
Not to be afraid of
falling
in love with someone like me.
And I imagined my words being absorbed
by your subconscious as your dreams
showed you what we could be together,
if you'd just listen to your heart and let me in.
But I never really got to whisper those words,
because I was too afraid,
too overwhelmed
by the realization of just how much
I really did love you.
That moment was so perfect, so beautiful,
and I could not help but cry because
my heart was and is so full of love for you that
there's no more room for anything or anyone anymore,
and it hurts.

Maybe you don't feel
as strongly as I do, but I know you
feel something.
So why do you always do this to me?
Why do you let me get so close,
close enough to feel you, to feel your love
and then push me
away?
You gave me the most precious gift
your love and a piece of your heart,
but then took it back
when it got too intense,
Too real,
Too close to your fantasy

and I wonder if it would've worked
had I whispered those words
"don't be afraid to love someone like me"
"Please, let yourself love me…"
"Please"

NO ONE CAN HOLD HER

Two men embraced
One woman
Who cannot be made whole
By just one.

The first, her chosen
Possessed her body and her mind
While the other,
Pure love found at last.
Dominates her heart and soul

Her mutilated body rests
In wastelands because of her chosen
While her true love now
Swaddles her scarred heart and soul
In his gentle touch

Two men embraced
One woman
And together they
Made her whole

But neither could really hold her
No one will ever hold her
No never, not ever, again.
The damage has gone too far.

AGAIN, I AM ALONE

I lie
naked on the sheets
the lived in apartment lights
peek in through the blinds
I wait
for a healing touch
his kiss
still fresh in my heart
I cry
waiting to feel him
so close
to me again

THE ONLY MAN I WILL EVER LOVE

All of my life, I've dreamed of someone like you to shower
with all my love.
Then one day, out of the blue, you stumbled into my life;
a gift from above.
When I looked into your eyes, I saw gentleness, kindness,
understanding
and a lifetime of safety and love with you.
But as quickly as the Universe gave you to me
It snatched you away.
And though now we spend our days apart, I alway carry you
in a special corner of my heart.
No one has ever touched me in the ways that you have;
no one ever will.
So, I gave you what I prized the very most --
I gave you my heart and the rest of my life to hold.
But the cruelty of life was made powerfully strong
As I learned that the rest of my earthly life wasn't to be
spent with you.
So now, now matter what this hell hold for me,
know this;
You alone are my love!
And it is always at your side that I remain.

SOMEONE TO HOLD ME WHEN I FALL…

Invisible tears role down my cheeks
As inwardly I cry almost all of the time
Until my life force is almost spent
I sit alone in this small "ghetto" building
Learning how family and friends really feel
I feel the loneliness
The emptiness
The fear
And there is no one who can help me; or really wants to
No one notices me when I walk by anymore
Few give me a genuine smile and only a "special little one"
makes me laugh
How in the world did I wind up in this hell,
Or should I ask why I deserve to be here?
Please, give me back a bit of my life
Let me forget the pain
Won't someone help me like I have helped them
So many times before?
Because, now, I **need** the help.
I need a friend
A companion I can trust
Somebody who will hold me when I'm falling
Somebody who will talk with me about everything
And listen as I talk in return
Someone who will not break a promise
Or leave me stranded with un-fulfilled dreams.
Are you what I long for?
Are you my family, my friend, my love?

I need a companion I can truly trust.

REFLECTIONS OF A LONGED FOR LOVE

(Doug)

I gaze into
the widows
of my soul.
I see you
looking back
at me.

My hand
reaches out...
But you're
not there.

I grasp
at emptiness.
My heart
breaks
at the thought that

I may not
find you.. and
You are
an illusion,
...created by my longing.

DISAPPEARING

I dare not ask,

but can't help but wonder

if thoughts of me invade your day

as they did not so long ago?

When gazing at the midnight sky

do you find comfort that I am blanketed

by the same bright stars?

Can you remember the taste of my lips

and do you still harden at the thought of me?

Because as days go by, my love and my life,

I must admit,

I fear I am disappearing.

A Soft Desert Breeze

The sun beats down upon me
Burning holes in my tranquility.
Barren were the plains,
Lost, stumbling, were my steps.
No stones marked my way,
No quiet voice stilled the pain.
My thoughts ran rampant;
Tumbleweeds blown by a hot, dry wind.

Then you came, a cool rain,
A soft breeze across the desert.
Gentle heart of spirit song
Singing to my loneliness.
You tenderly passed through me,
Whispered light of peace,
Breath of ancient Celtic wisdom
In your moon's reflected glow.

AFTER DARK

(A Widow's Lonely Night)

After dark
the sound of silence
plagues my naked ear
The sound of lovers
sharing passionate embraces
echoes in the starlit sky.

After dark, the night
is my blanket of silence.
It protects me from my fears and
all of my nightmares.

After dark, I sit staring at the full moon,
tears streaming down my soft cheeks,
dreaming of the perfect you.
Listening to the silence,
After dark.

BRIDAL BOUQUET

Sunshine yellow center
Melting warmly over
Soft white petals
Of nature's pure consistency

Picked just for her
They now lay dying
In the warmth of her own hands
Constant never more

ALONE

Things are so bad here now
There's nothing here for me
I gave it all away
Lived my beliefs and loved as hard as I could

Now, I'm so unresolved
No one understands what it feels like
I have a list of regrets that just keeps getting longer
And no one to hold me as I try to let them go.

I'll finally leave the same way I came
Totally alone and out of place
While everyone I'd hoped would stand by me
Disappeared or turned away.

All my insecurities keep getting confirmed
Why's it so hard to be near me?
The last twelve years have apparently been a waste
Putting out one fire or another for family or friend or even foe.

Now, I'll leave the same way I came
And after 5 months I'll be forgotten
There's something deathly wrong with me
I can't even pretend to be okay, not anymore

My nightmare, my late husband's prophecy, is coming true
Eyes that once smiled at me just turn away
And it doesn't matter how many tears I cry
No one cares, they have what they want
And I am useless now. He said it would be that way.

Tell me why you just throw me away?
How did I let your down or disappoint you?
I tried to do my best and love you in all things.
Now, I'm never lonelier than when you are in the room!

But it doesn't matter . . .
Ashes to ashes
Dust to dust

I'm leaving the way I came
Alone

AM I LOSING YOU?

Your love is leaving me now
like day turning into night.
I struggle to find some way, somehow,
to rekindle our love, it has been my only light.

This dark and lonely night
I sit and wait for your call.
But there's nothing here except my lamplight,
and the reflections on my wall.

I'm missing you more deeply,
With a passion never known.
And logic fights my senses
On why you left me all alone.

I love you so intensely,
More than you will ever know.
As loss and depression cover densely
What little hope I had allowed to grow.

LOST

Here I sit, lost in thoughts
of the way things used to be.
Not of the smiles, or the tears
But of the simple being of him and me...
Not of the days, nor the nights
nor the autumn leaves that blew away;
But of the times we spent together, alone
Of the love that now lies in ashes on a tray.

I ponder the moments He held me close
I believed every word He said.
Not like the stories, nor the fairy-tales
But more real than any of those I had read.
Not like the nightmares of childhood, nor the dreams,
but of a different sense
Before the engulfing pain that followed the death
I remember that love, so intense.

But getting lost leads to disjointed thoughts,
and finally the time has come when I must think all this through
This moment that was given to walled up emotion and memory
Can no longer hide what is real and true.
The pain of His leaving still resonates deep inside;
The tears today fall in a steady pace
And for 2,955 days the sun has been replaced with night
Since the day I lost his love and embrace.

For far too long I failed to see flowers bloom
Nor hear the lullaby's of sleep
No fairy-tales were read aloud
And today, in ash, I regret the promise I failed to keep.
Tonight, I will not fear the nightmares
I will bathe in my recent dreams
And although I am not really alone
For this one night, I will fully fall apart at the seams.

And after all is said and done
I no longer still believe
the words he said so concise that night.
The pent up feelings I could never share or achieve
Are pouring out, in gratitude, love and relief.
I hate to look back on the past
With such regret and shame
But today, as I finally lose and find myself.
I find I have only me to blame.

TODAY I SENT YOU HOME

(for Doug)
Alone in the garden of memory,
Where our children said their vows
dying rose petals swirl in patterns of red and white,
from stems heavy with the promise of winters rest.
The cloying scent of a desert autumn fills the air,
mixed with the spicy scent of sage.
I think of you as you were.
Strong arms and gentle hands stroking your guitar
Eyes closed, as you became part of the rhythm and the words.
Your back bare and stretched,
the sinew of your arms flexing
with each movement of your fingers
as your hands traveled the frets of your guitar.
I wanted you most
when you weren't aware of my presence,
delved into playing your music with dedication.
Too bad you did not see…

Today I stand in a red rock forest,
in the shadow of Cathedral Rock
spill your ashes into a flowing creek
and do not weep.

AND NOW YOU ARE GONE

I will never be able
to describe
the wonder and the overwhelming
warmth and feeling
of connection that I
gained with you as I lay
there naked beside you in your
strong arms.

never would words do it justice,
but I feel like I have to try,
or else that perfect moment will fade
like so many photographs in my memory,
that the realness of it will
turn into some kind of a dream,
that the feeling of not knowing
where I ended
and you began
will be floated into some kind
of mist into a place
where the depth of the waters
murky-up the clarity of the memory
you try so hard not to lose
sight of.

Your face that morning I
see every time I close my eyes.
Your soft, even breathing,
eyes closed, lips so gently parted,
innocent, almost pouting,
your insecurity coming to the surface,
angel-faced, blue eyed boy.
And I wrapped myself around you,
half to keep you from slipping away,
half to pull you as close to me
as possible without becoming two
in one being.

And now you are gone
Did I hold on to you too tightly?
Or was my grasp so gentle
That I let you slip through
And lost you to yourself?

HE CALLED TO TELL ME

It seems we've run aground
(he called to tell me)
well that's quite all right
just don't lose faith in me
even though I've gone away.

My problem isn't you
(he called to tell me)
it's just the things I do
that are driving me to drink and drug
just let me have my way
let me go away for a while

I don't love you less
(he called to tell me)
when I am not around
we're just on shaky ground
and I need some time to rest

The stars will realign
(he called to tell me)
all in the proper time
I'll find you when I'm better
so stop trying to fix me!

Don't worry my love
(I answered him)
I already have...

DRIFTED SOUL

Her soul walks among strangers,
A graveyard where no one exists.
Within her soul- there's only blackness,
Long ago she lost the light.

Trying to figure out life's rhyme and reason,
(to escape from where the dead come alive.)
In the unknown, she wanders
In a world of her own; pain eats her entire soul.

'Hurt' no longer feeds the heart.
A heart that has given up trying.
Trying to break stone can be hard
when there's no faith in your belief.

Her hope has disappeared, where no logic reigns.
Within an empty room, a journal and her losses,
Poetry no longer makes sense,
Words only feed the hatred for the world being cruel.

Neglecting warmth from someone sincere,
Due to the past hurts which brought her here.
Life's the enemy- break away,
She seeks a distance in her mind,

Only she can travel to the other side.
Overcome the betrayals from every angle in her heart.
Her image is strong, but her body is weak.
Trembling heart, stumbling feet,

Blood like tears now falls from her eyes,
(smash that mirror and run.)
Can't feel safe in a world that's dead,
a wilderness of mirrors
life can't exist outside her head.

Her hope now gone, her feelings turned cold.
She can no longer fight on.
Towards the beach, she climbs the rocks.
Inhales the breeze... she screams.

She SOARS high in to the sky,
Now, she's free to fly...

THEN YOU CAN LEAVE

wrap me in your arms
hold me tight
please don't let go
warm me to my toes
fill me with love once again
block my fears and tormentors too
I need to be with you
surrounded by your arms
tightly holding me up
firm with love and understanding
stir the love within once again
a hug is all I ask
you can leave after that
just one more hug,
is it really too much to ask?

Happy Birthday My Love

(October 17, 2000)
I keep saying
"it would have been"
your birthday.
But today IS your birthday.
We will still celebrate
that day
so many years ago
when you were born,
but it will be a bitter-sweet celebration
without you.
I will allow myself to feel happy
on this your special day,
to be happy for the life you had
(and so selflessly shared with me).
I'll try to imagine that
you are at peace, pain free and happy now.
I'll try as hard as I can.
With your children and a new love to guide me,
for through them you are here with me now.
As we celebrate the gift of life; the day of your birth.

MOMENTS NOT TAKEN

Another fall and winter are behind us
Yet another long spring and summer lie ahead
So many things not done
So many things not said

"Maybe tomorrow"...
That's the phrase I have come to hate
Our next moment's are not even guaranteed
What is tomorrow is too late?

My heart cries for the tomorrows
And the next weeks that will never come
As I look ahead and wonder,
Why has it always been this way?

Moments lost in prioritizing
Putting my work before play,
Forgetting my need for love in the chaos,
Trusting on the next moment, next hour, next day.

If I had only loved like there's no tomorrow
Lived like there's only today,
Basked in the glow of each moment
Maybe I would not regret my yesterdays

If we could live by those simple ideas.
Adopt them as our new creed,
There'd be no more lost moments
And all hearts would be freed.

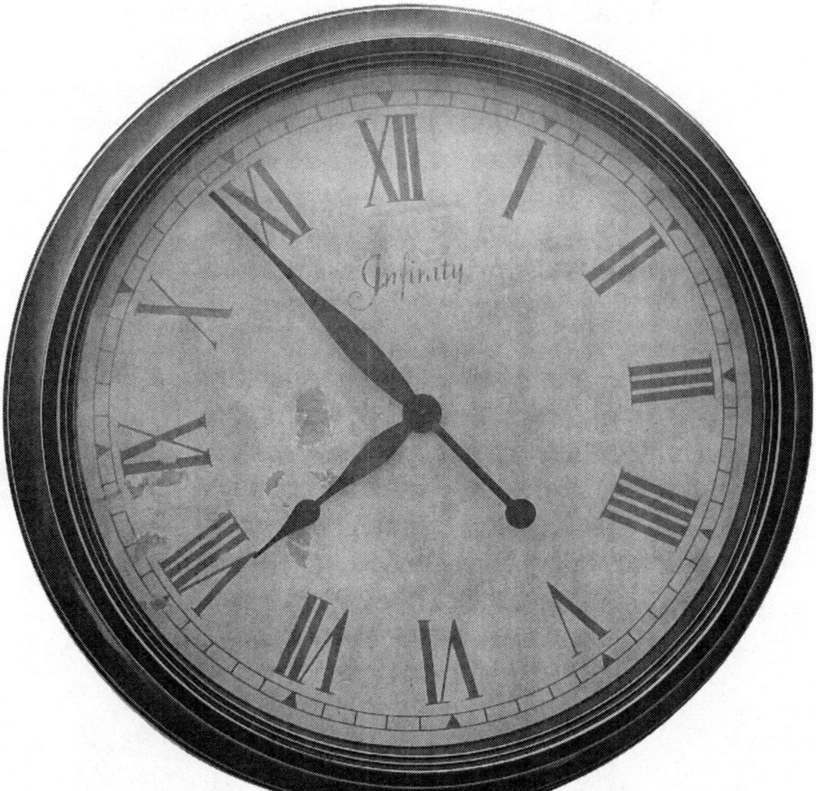
Infinity

HER LOST LOVE

Feeling the wrath of a broken love,
she is torn between the lines
of future responsibilities and needs.
She carries the weight of a broken heart
and a wounded soul.

A tear slips from her faded blue eyes.
She tries to act like she hasn't been affected,
but the way her eyes look so dull
tells the world she is devastated.
Her laughter, so weak and unsure,
tells everyone she doesn't know where to go now.
Her touch, so cold and rough,
lets the world know she has now become
her worst nightmare.

Her dreams turned into her nightmares,
her fears turned into her reality.
Her lost love haunts her every waking hour,
her lost love is only what she can see now.
Her lost love has left her broken,
her unending love has left her with nothing.
She has lost her dream love,
a lost love, never to be found...
Her lost love.

CAPTIVE DOVE

I remember the pigeon
The fledgling I held in hand
Whose parents had forced it from its nest
Before it could fly
Or fend
Desperately struggling
In my gentle grasp
His body convulsed
And yet I denied
His right to freedom
And held him in a cage
Until he could survive
And face the world alone
Not knowing what his future would even hold.

And now,
What protest can or will alter
What time and fate brings to any of us
Like it did to that sweet bird
I held in captive love?

As for me…
Your scent is fading
From the gown I last wore when
I slept beside you
And felt so safe and secure

Your smile
And hazel eyes
Vanish in a haze of tears
Flooding from my eyes.

I have forever been expelled
From your past
And yet, my heart is bound
Forever to what is not
And probably never will be

I lift my glass of worm wood
To numb my own internal interrogations
Of another cold hearted night
Waiting
Like a hostage
Like that fledging rock dove
For Apollo's first golden flames
To release me from these rising and falling thoughts...

Then, I will throw myself into the abyss.

LET ME ATONE

a warm sunset slides in glorious red
slow motion, love dances in my head
bright lovers moon, slowly on the rise
velvet backdrop, luminescent star filled skies
this warm and breezy Saturday night
all in the glow of apartment street lights
as I stare out my window, all alone,
wishing my true love to come home
missing you, that other part of me
something I started, and wished so much to be

on glass reflected, loves sad face
so lost without your special place
candle glows, my face and tears
pain of love lost, seems like years
in reality, a single day has passed
since, with barely a word, I saw you last
a lesson of love, so hard to learn
love played, leaves, once spurned
stop pride, games of love for fun
how complete, your love has won

this love, a lifetime my soul did seek
a tender love within kindness speaks
comfort from longing, with kissed tears
my lovers deep kiss to banish fears
dreams of caress, love and romance
my desire delayed, now held in trance
so, captured in this web of love he spun
only fools believe that true love's for fun
wish your return with every fiber in me
to tell how sorry I am, how wise I will be

radiant dawn, spires across the sky
my broken heart does weep and cry
such a fool I was not to be content alone
Hear me Goddess!
Please, let my love hear me atone.

LOVES NEVER TO BE SHARED

He died...
He is gone...
And still the morning comes
Demanding that I go on

He was taken from me
Taken too soon
From the damaged woman who loved...
Who loves...

Is he really in heaven somewhere?
Is he happier in his new home?
He seemed so unhappy here.
I hope his pain is done

My selfish tears still fall
And unceasingly I cry
Every anniversary
A memory of the day he died
A memory of loves never to be shared.
A memory of a life that was, maybe, after all a lie.

I send that love to my man above
The love that keeps his memory ever alive
In my heart, in my soul, and in my thoughts.
A memory that keeps him by my side

I cannot say "farewell my love"
I can't face the emptiness it would mean
Or the reality that says
I must walk this last mile
Alone
With a memory of loves never to be shared.

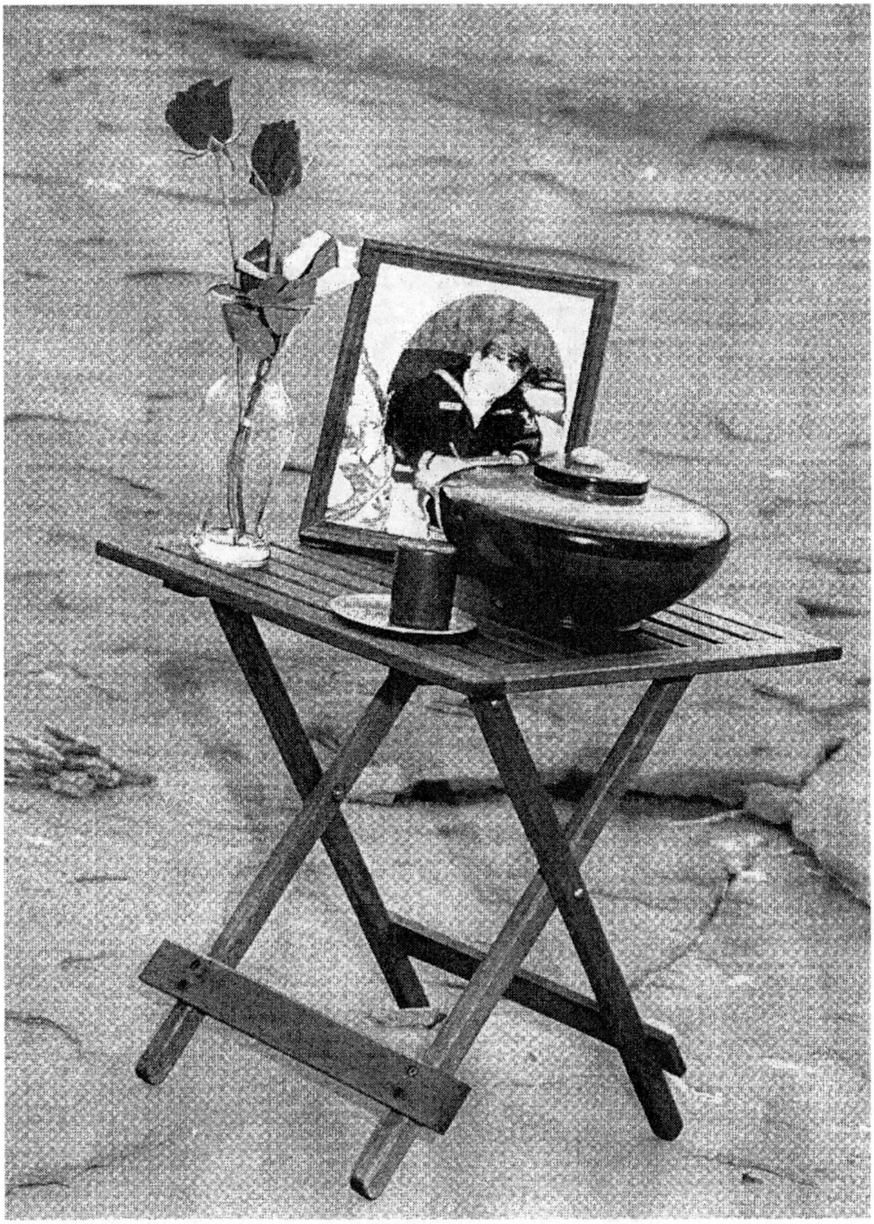

MY FOREVER LOVE

my forever-lasting love
my never-ending pain
you... a sign of eternity
my leader to infinite senselessness

awaiting to live my life (forever yours)
while my soul is being blazed to the core
in the grief of your departure
crying very loud, cries heard by everyone but you

you, new-loved, plod to the top of the hill
pretending I never existed in your life
how can that be?, without you I'd never had existed at all
my life is frozen in the broken past-time of us

past-time which laid in doom, destined to die to soon
now sorrow will be my name
and I will be banished to my own hell
this hell, not solely of my own making, where you sent me to dwell

You filled me with joy then sent me to damnation
damnation that turned on your love's dying embers
those embers are my painful poison
poison, running all over through my veins

reaching my heart, reaching my soul
hunting my being, bringing me to death
But, I will thank you as my last breath draws near
For life has lost its essence... it has lost you.

Peace

(for Douglas Pike)

Dreaming of sunsets,
of sugar white sands
it seems as though
I feel the ocean spray
the waves roll slowly in,
a gull glides by.
I whisper into the wind
A lifetime of memories
flow through my mind
and then...

I think of my lost love
and smile.

Photograph

Memories of you and me
Tumble inside my head
The way it used to be
The things you said
No one else has ever
Made me believe so strong
You left me to wonder
How did my love go wrong?
I lie awake at night
And wait for the sun to shine.
I still feel you next to me,
Your lips on mine.
Without a warning
You made our love a lie.
You said you were sorry,
But you never told me why.
Maybe my love is in vain
Maybe you're the hurting kind
I can't take any more of this pain
I've got to get you off my mind
I tried to be what you wanted
I gave you all I had
But you left me with nothing
Nothing but this photograph
And my shattered spirit.

LUPINE WOMAN

Candles burn, flicker and flash
whispered voices, fill my head
vows taken in the caress
wishes granted, deals made.

He came to me upon a dream
long ago, took my hand
called me child
said we would talk
and he said the reality
 I would be loved always
by him
From that day there was no more,
nothing left of innocence lost
gladly taken, forever lost
from time to time
he returns his call
just to remind me
I gave it all

music screaming in my head
songs of torture fear and dread
all my gifts he gave to me
have left me with
cold brutality ..
Barren heart, soul so lost
little girl, lupine angel
woman child forever lost
I wander alone now
ever the huntress
incapable of stopping
the beast I have become
tempting death
awaiting his caress
to end the madness
only to be denied his arrival.
Mental monsters seek out my insanity

coupling with vengeance
ice flowing through my veins
I chuckle at the pain
for I feel only the hunger
dreaming of crimson rainstorms
the quest never done

LOOK CLOSELY

Sure but subtle
The music infiltrates through the barriers
That confine the most precious of memories
To release them
And expose them
In their grandest nakedness

bequeathed by concern
they are worshiped and loved
gently handled and softly caressed

purged by force
they are hated and despised
rudely mangled and obscenely viewed

When the music is gone
Silent and forgotten
they retreat easily
But cold
Back to their prisons of finality

Waiting
For the turning of the record
That they may be exhumed
And again live
Always uncertain
For brief periods of existence

If you look closely
Those
Are not
Tears of joy

AN IRONING BOARD NAMED MIKE

For years she had pressed, starched
And creased dress whites
So that he could shine on the inspection line
 And maybe make a new rate.
A four "0" appearance would mean more money
More activities for the kids
Another university course
Maybe even a lover's dinner
From time to time.

The heat of the iron, the smell of starch
The rhythmic motions
Back and forth
Back and forth
Often helped to soothe her.

A navy wife spent many hours alone
Waiting, working, wanting.
Lengthy sea tours
Long nights of "duty"
Made many nights seem long and foreboding

That is when she would iron
Iron her husband's uniforms
Catch a brief smell of his cologne
As the heat touched the cloth
That touched his skin, that touched her own.

Now, she irons for no one but herself
Still the familiar ironing board brings solace
From her sense of loss
A husband dead, a wife bereft.
So she irons to maintain her sanity

She even named the ironing board
After her long lost mate.
At least she can still be near him
Talk to him that way
Via her ironing board called Mike

THE AUTUMN OF HER DAYS

I walk the autumn path of life alone in my remaining years
And think of all the seasons we once knew,
When hand in hand we walked together,
Beneath suns of cloudless blue.

Oh, how we loved to watch the seasons change,
to feel the breath of life carried in the very air,
But now the way is dark and strange;
The bitter chill is more than I can bear.

I cannot see a multicolored show
of dancing leaves resplendent in display,
for somber is the color that I know,
so lifeless and lonely is the autumn of my days.
I long to see the leaves in flaming hue,
To feel your arms strong and secure,
and walk the path again with you.

WANTING YOU

Every day I mourn for you
I long to feel your touch
I cry myself to sleep at night
From wanting you so much

I wonder if this pain will ever go away
It's been hurting me so long
And I long to be with you
And help right all those wrongs

Life drags on without you
Nothing but emptiness inside
I wonder how long I will have to wait
To have you at my side

It does not matter how long it is
Or how far I have to go
I will love you till forever is gone
And that you have to know

And when that "forever" morning comes
How happy I will be!
Oh, I hope it is true
Finally, and forever, I will be back with you

THE SILVER CHORD

(Doug)

Yama has carried your soul away
Physically depriving me of your touch
Your scent
The sound of your voice
Which often bubbled
Like an underground brook
Or raged like a hurricane whipped ocean.
Still we remain bound together
As one, from the beginning of time,
From this lifetime to the next,
By a thin luminous ribbon
Only angels, true believes, and God can see.
Woven at the dawning of space and time by sacred spiders
Spinning thin strands of silver pulled from a star filled universe,
And anointed and made holy by Gods and Goddesses
Whose names are no longer spoken but felt
In the hearts of those who love eternally.
It carries a current of mysterious influence
Which binds two souls, two hearts, throughout eternity:
Well past the gates of a heaven or a hell.
A silver chord, which will lead like soul to like soul as
Each returns to the earth mother to be reborn again;
One only to the other.
This silver string is the beam of sun-split truth that leads
The lost empty soul to its new mate, giving it peace,
Breathing life into each one again
Each able to give and receive joy for another brief eon
Bound permanently by the Silver Chord.

MOONCAST

Across diamond dust beaches
licked tentatively by silver tongues
of salt sea spray
a lonely water sprite
frolics under a canopy of stars
beckoning Orion to leave his throne
and join her in passion's dance.

As the western sun slowly rises
a moon cast shadow covers the earth
silhouetting two silk white immortals
glistening in the dew
whose souls have intertwined
in an embrace of love
blessed by Jupiter himself.

IMAGE

I sit in my closet
Curled in a fetal form,
going through old letters
containing so many secrets,
reading old notes
looking through pictures
that were left to be forgotten,
trying to forget the memories
that still haunt me in my sleep,
his familiar face reminds me of so much,
I had tried to bury him in my mind
before the fire turned his sweet body to ash,
I should have gone too,
I was not supposed to outlive him.

After he died,
I come across this note,
his named signed at the bottom,
oh, the memories we had,
and when I turned,
the image of that familiar face
Gazed at me through haunted eyes.

LONGING

Alone I sit and listen
to the sounds of emptiness
singing to me,
The one with empty arms
and broken dreams

Everything I ever wanted, seems
unreachable or taken by another
Is fate a cruel prankster, with an unfunny joke?

I wonder at times, if destiny
has deemed me to wander all alone
never knowing a lovers caress, or the passion in his eyes

at times the longing is maddening
the tears fall and melt into my pillow
the loneliness enveloping me once again
I curse my longing soul

I watch others and still can smile at their joy
but at times, the hurt is raw
a reminder of what I don't have
and maybe never will

No lovers laughter or knowing smiles
no cuddles in the break of day light
my words heard whispered in the darkness
only by my Goddess and me

so many broken dreams , promises
all came to me times past,
but do nothing in the now
for now I am alone in my bed and life
with unanswered songs

never touching the realness
of a lovers face and hair
only staring at the space of nothing
and feeling more alone then I ever believed I could

Never did I imagine I would end up this way
to end each day hungering for the touch
of the one I love
But he isn't here
The one for which I long.

Screaming in my mind,
Shattering my heart like broken glass,
I am tired of all alone
I face alone the day in my cold bed
A nocturnal bird of prey all alone
in the void of emptiness that is my world

A Prussian Warrior's Love

For Tom Fernow

Resplendent in his uniform
He stands on the battlefield of life
Knowing that he'll live or die
By the mighty sword he wields

Some people fight for honor
Some people fight for fame
Most people fight to stay alive
Just to make it home again

People shouted that the war was on
That most dreaded of all cries
They forced him to leave his happy home
Because things in the world had gone awry

He made a promise to return
When he kissed his lady good-bye
He swore this would be the last time
That he would answer their battle cry

Now in the midst of battle
He fights for limb and life
Anxious to go home again
Longing to end this nomadic strife

He has always been a warrior
And he thought he'd die as such
But her love gives him an inner peace
That nothing else can touch....

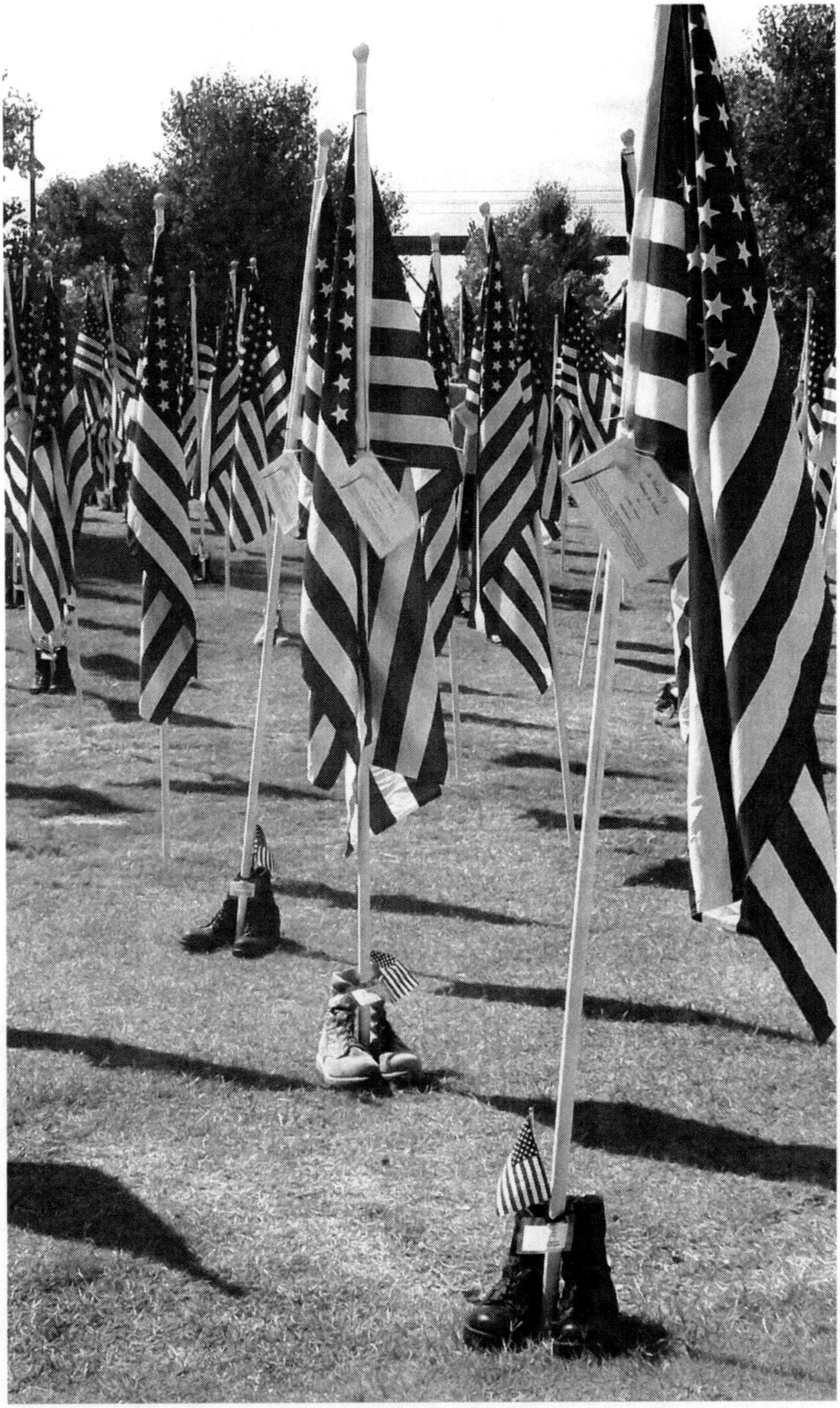

SWEET MEMORIES

(For Tom)

The night falls silently
Like a dark veil covering the earth
It is the end of my day…
Another day without you

Not a moment goes by that you are not on my mind
Oh, how I wish I could be with you now
The days drift by slowly like sand in the hourglass of time
I count the moments until we are together again
Knowing they will be infinite.

A warm gentle breeze begins to blow
And for a moment, I could swear I hear you calling my name
Quietly whispering into my ear
I turn, only to realize, one again, that you are not there
I dream while wide awake.

Another lonely night without you
Tears begin to drench my pillows
Accompanied by the aching of a broken heart
Torn by the memories of you and our time together

The smile on your face and the taste of your lips
Forever branded upon my memories
I am haunted endlessly by the thought of you
But it is not the memories I desire, it's you…only you

Did you know that the moment we met, my life changed forever
Never before has anyone touched my heart such as you
You rekindled the embers that I thought had died long ago
And created a fire deep within my soul making me feel.

All that I am now and will ever be is because of you
You are the strength that guides me every hour of every day
The memories of you can never be replaced
Memories…. sweet memories…. memories of you

THE ROPE

(for Ellen Christine Capurso)

the mountains echo your name
the sun and moon whisper your name
in your dreams
you wake to live
to breathe
to feel
the rope is thrown to you
yet, you're afraid to grasp
a thread of friendship
broken so easy
like so many times before
you reach
GRASP
and you fall
into a dark cavern
and you're alone
CRYING OUT
not in voice
but in soul
torn...with heart
the smile you give
is a grimace

Please
don't shed a tear
the rope will hold
the mountains will echo with love
and the tears you shed
will be dried
from the hand of this woman
this friend

capture this single moment
don't be afraid of this rope
a lifeline
not every rope breaks
just hold on
hold on
hold on ..to me
forever.

LESSONS OF THE DRAGONFLY

For Maggie O'Donnell Froncek

It batted through the web
before I could run back,
tangling the dragonfly, and then
to the ground, where it flailed about
full of grit and bits of leaves.
My immediate need was to rescue it
and sighing I thought of other rescue attempts,
for the co worker I know
who's father was dying now,
for my daughter's second god father
who died gallantly in a long ago November
for my late husband who slipped away
far too soon
for my own life again
in the sticky threads of cancer and fate
.

Biting my lip
I sent for sharp scissors,
the dragonfly clung to my finger, here comes the
bite I thought, but it only settled submissively,
chewing instead at a chunk of web
while I snipped and held breath,
eased each strand from the wings,
the incredibly delicate wings,
dreading the moment I would tear them
or slip the scissors blade.

It curled its abdomen up
and rested there
and although I ached for its flight
I left it alone, not wanting to watch ,
its death or deliverance not wanting to dwell on
 others I could not be help to live.

Later, when I saw that it had flown
I wished we could have spoken
Could it tell me it was grateful?
Could I tell myself?
Of how inevitably we work
to free ourselves
from each particular ordeal,
Of all the wonder and surprise,
held in hands that free us
with precision and with tenderness.
Of the precious gift of life
Of love.

The Truth About Nobody's Child

He always called her his "china doll"
And said he had clumsy hands.
Yet those hands held her so tenderly
That, had she been china,
She would have slipped through his grasp
And shattered to pieces against the floor of life;
Still nobody's child with a stone cold heart.

No china doll, this nobody's child.
Life has pummeled the stuffing out of her.
Yet still there is enough love within
For others to cling to, and draw from,
gain comfort from, as they feel the blows of life.
Her little red heart always says Love
Because nobody's child is a "raggedy doll"

ONLY YESTERDAY

(For Gary Lemcke)

Only yesterday it seems
We sat in this same fashion
Acne prone teens
Eager to explore
Every facet of love
That first kiss
Still gives me something
To lose sleep over

Parents ourselves now,
We gaze back and forth
Each in turn wondering
How the years escaped us
A little heavier on the outside
Our faces long clear of acne
Showing the first signs of aging
And, hidden between those lines,
The scars of buried loves.
Never old
Always in the process of healing.

Over a glass of wine
We laugh
We reminisce
We talk of deep pain
Cautiously optimistic
That love will find us each again
And keep our dying souls alive.

LOVE IN FLIGHT

(The heart of the hawk)

For James Bosworth

She unfolds
and releases herself
above the chasm
Fear's temptation
Hope's divide
so deceptively narrow,
so impossibly wide,
She yearns to follow
to reach the consecrated ground
on the other side.

She covets a piece
of his strong wings,
a crumb
of his courage,
a speck of his heart
(forgive her greed)
and pushes off
headfirst
into the void--

For a moment lovers hang
held up by the air
grasping
at the golden blood in the sun--

A select few
soar upward
on the cosmic wind--

Others
rain down
like rosary beads of colored glass
into that bitter black soup
where Icarus
faltered in his dream;

Oh how the white light entrances!
the radiant heat
She craves
She senses
the mountains fiercely

Pulling

a lifetime
can happen
in that moment,
while
suspended
in
the lover's sky.

EBB TIDES

(for Bob M)

The tide comes in, and moves back out
Like your chest rising and falling
To the melodic rhythm of your life

In the mist of the sea's dew
I see the future of our understanding love
Two old souls discovering the truth

Sand and shells shift underneath
Realizing the changes that have taken place
I know now . . . where my heart belongs

WE ARE (still) FRIENDS
(For Kim Wright Pritt)

We are friends
Walking arm in arm down these wide streets of life
Laughing, chatting, hoping, dreaming
Sharing those deep existential talks
And oft times leaving better than when we came.

I am deeply, darkly amused
But more deeply cut by my first initiation rite
With darkness, jealousy and hard-repressed fears
Lurking only too close beneath the surface
Prodding me to evil doing with their prickly vines.

We are friends
Walking down these dim-lit streets so late into the night
Streetlights cast frightful shadows upon our lineaments
Suddenly terrible under profundity's gaze
We walk together,
Haloed angels with devilish grins.

LIKE NOVEMBER FOLIAGE

I am exhausted from this internal struggle,
and the insidious disease called loneliness
so I sit and ponder if I should
have taken this blade to
my wrist many years
ago.

My soul withers with the
inner torment of how
people tend to ignore each other
or pleas for assistance.
Sometimes I feel as if
the world has just been out to take everything from
me.

Other times, I feel the world
would be better off without me.
That nothing I have ever done has made a difference
Or possibly I'm just
a waste of empty space.
I find I have nothing to more to care
about.

I do not have the great love
of my life that I promised
myself when I was a romantic.
I do not have a dream or a glimmer
of hope when I was a young woman.
All I do have is the overwhelming
sense of fear now running through my
blood.

So many times I have turned the
cold release of the razor before me.
So many times I pleaded with
hope to secure my fate.
So many times I desired to
be released from a world of struggle and
pain.

Only to wind up here, sitting alone in a sea of
empty hopes and dreams.

my optimistic shell is slowly
scattered around me like
the November foliage I kicked my way
through as a young
girl.

Those dried, fragrant leaves,
that carpeted the lawns,
provided a fantasy mountain cave
cushioned my tired body at rest,
or designed an artist's palate when pressed
between waxen sheets that now grace my wall
but ultimately made a beautiful funeral
 pyre.

DAMAGED DOVE

softly blows the wind
as the sky whispers
come my damaged child,
come to me

spreading battered wings
fragile membranes torn in envy
as they tried to force me
into their form
tried to hold me down forevermore.
but I escaped!
they did not win
I refused to let them

they tried to steal my spirit
"you will never soar again"
they whispered cruelly
as they chained my broken body
but they could not bind my mind
my thoughts flew free
for the sky did not forget
her stolen daughter

my mangled wings
will always hang in shreds
they can never carry me
to dizzying heights
but I still see my dreams
hung in the tree tops

it is enough that I fly once again
and they can no longer touch me

FAMILY BEGINNINGS

(FOR MY D.,J.,DE.,AND M.)

It's morning,
She descends the cold, quiet
Stairwell
Relishing the serenity of this
Special time;
Her world alone.

Coffee's on.
The bitter, inviting aroma wafts
Upward
To the bedroom where he sleeps still;
Snoring vigorously.

He rises.
Awakened gently by the call of her
Soft voice.
He stumbles down to greet her
Warmly
In love's embrace.

Breakfast's ready.
With a volcanic voice
He beckons
Rousing three "angelic" beings
from heaven's plains.
They come.
Warm from slumber's peaceful
Caresses.
The proof of their all-powerful love.
The circles complete.

Kisses given,
She bids these rays of life
Good-bye,
Then patiently prepares for their
Return at end of day.

DOUGLAS

(my oldest)
When they first lay you in my arms that day,
I didn't want to give in to required sleep
I knew those rosy cheeks and baby sounds
Were something I would not get to keep
Because

Baby boys grow up … much too soon

I closed my eyes for a short sweet nap
Only to wake and find
A "big boy" instead of the infant
That I had once cradled
Because

Baby boys grow up … much too soon

I kept watch as long as I could
Knowing what would occur
But sleep did come again and when it left
Twenty years had passed by in a blur
Because

Baby boys grow up … much too soon

Now instead of those fat rosy cheeks
When I look at my grown son, I see
A young man with the same blue eyes
As the baby he used to be
Because

Baby boys grow up... much too soon.
The laughter of childhood has been replaced
With responsibility, duty, and care
Those blue eyes show with worry now
But still the sparkle's there
My baby boy grew up… much, much too soon.

And I find I love him even more.

CAROUSEL CARILLONS OF CHILDHOOD'S END

A mystical carousel
My mind's eye still sees
Filled with the joys
Of childhood's reveries

Of colorful stallions
Spinning round and round
From which a small boy's laughter
Will forever resound

Spurring him on
To a carillon battle field
Where he fights holy wars
And his foes always yield

Until the carousel stops
Its tumultuous spin
And reality's tides
Come rushing in.

An ancient carousel
My mind's eye still sees
Filled with precious joys
Now held precariously

Of a fantasy child
Grown a troubled young man
Too big to be carried
To a carillon land.

Too weary of fighting
The foes that won't yield
The sword at his side
Now too heavy to wield.

The carousel's tune
Haunts me daily still
With memories of hope
The passing years slowly kill.

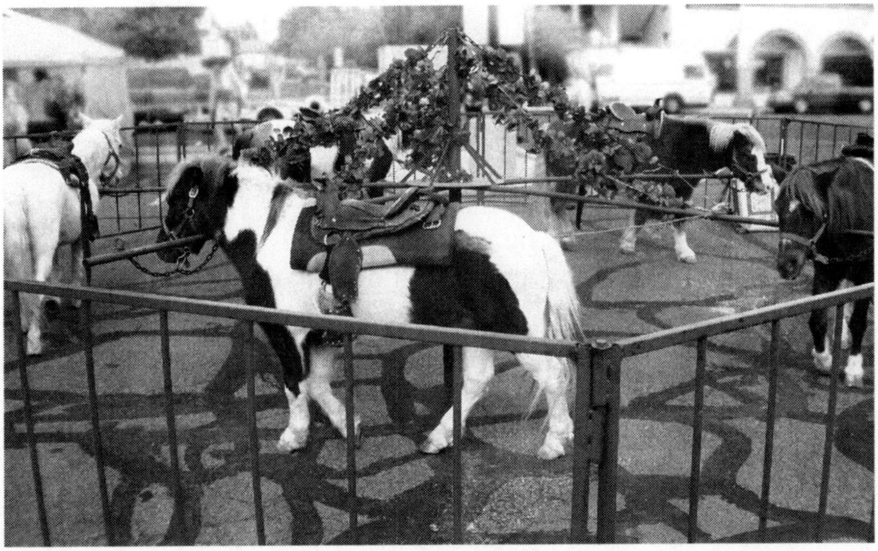

FIRST DANCE

(For James)

Feeling ancient and lifeless,
I went to visit his today
and renew my memories of yesterday.

Mesmerized, I watched him
laughing,
living.

I melted into a darkened corner
in fear of being seen.
He sought me out in that blackness.

Eyes full of wisdom,
A heart full of love,
He escorted me to the dance floor

We danced,
a slow dance.
Our first.

My soul filled with pride
as I gazed into the eyes
of this handsome young man;

My twelve-year-old son.

MARY

My little girl has grown up now
Quite beautifully,
As anyone with eyes can plainly see
And, she has a daughter of her own now
That thought touches a special, hidden part of me

Is she a good Mother?
Rest assured, yes!
She learned her lessons well
Bouncing back to persevere
Every time she fell

Raising her own little girl
Wrapped in love abounding
Reminding her of her childhood days
The life she lived before

Some things we never realize
Until our own kids start to grow
Then, we simply pause and smile
Silently saying "I told you so".

So listen to your Mother, child
A strange, strong woman for sure
Because the pearls of wisdom she once spoke
Will be a truth that will forever will endure

CATCH THE MORNING STAR!

(for my Jessica; a fellow stargazer)

So within this race called life
I soon will find
The light of the moon
Others also left behind
Trying to free their immortal souls
By catching the morning star...

Now that the time
Has come and gone
Illusions have past
And I am on my own
Know that I will never be far...
You will see me again
When you, too, catch the Morning Star.

MOM-MOM'S LOVE

(The promise I can't keep)

Tiny footsteps padding softly down the hall
Moving very quickly, like a slinky, covert cat
Slipping through the dimness toward the light
The query, "where is my Mom-Mom at?"

Pretending not to notice, I continue with my studies
A shuffling in the corridor, causes me to steal a peek
Tousled, rumbled hair, drowsy, sleepy eyes
Lurking in the shadows, appearing very meek.

Clearing from my throat a pretentious little lump
I gently close my book, appearing nonchalant
In a faint and fretful voice, the visitor proclaims
"Sitting with my Mom-Mom is truly what I want."

Feigning grave surprise, a gasp I let escape
I hear giggling from the shadows, but not a move she makes
Powerless to prolong my ridiculous charade
I open my arms wide, will this be the cue she takes?

The delicate little fairy floats across the room
Limbs extended out toward me, a beam upon her face.
She hurls herself upon me, wriggles nearer yet
A sigh seeps from her lips, as I enfold her in my embrace.

Angelic features radiant, warm breath upon my cheek
A sleepy, wispy line she speaks, and I begin to weep,
"Promise when I wake, you will be here just for me?"
"I love you very much, you know"
And she tumbles off to sleep.

The Lap Waiting Just For You.

The bed time lullabies and stories
with mom-mom next to you
as we cuddled together in bed
me stroking your hair making you feel safe and important

Running around with mom-mom right behind
as I grab you in a blanket covered hug

The lap that is always open with a seat just for you,
watching musicals that never get old

The lap that is always open, with a seat just for you
The lap that is always open.... waiting just for you.

THE LINGERIE DRAWER

(For my daughter and granddaughter; Mary and Jessica)

The drawers, lined with scented paper
Of lavender and rose,
Show no sign of the woman
Who flirted, laughed, and loved.
Who held the hearts of boys
In playful hands
And finally captured her lover's heart.

Ancient photos show glimpses
Of lace and silk
Of garters and corsets
Which encased a beauty's body,
Hers,
In satin and velvet.
But the drawers, now, show only cavernous comfort

A few cotton bras and panties,
A girdle or two,
A flannel nighty,
And one of polyester in bold floral print;
Something surely only a grandmother must now wear.

Her outer shell remains pretty,
And this woman still shops the
"Secret" stores
And fills her daughter's drawers,
Now lined with lavender and rose,
With secret items of lace and silk
Of satin and velvet
And with scents of sandalwood and primrose.
Passing secrets of love and longing
To a budding generation

The woman's lingerie drawers
Tell the story of her life
Now nearly over
Her daughter's tell of the legacy
She will now leave behind
And one day, the daughter's daughter
Will view *her* aging mother's drawers
And wonder where *that* pretty, sensual woman went
But, if either look into a mirror
They will see the mother's mother staring back.

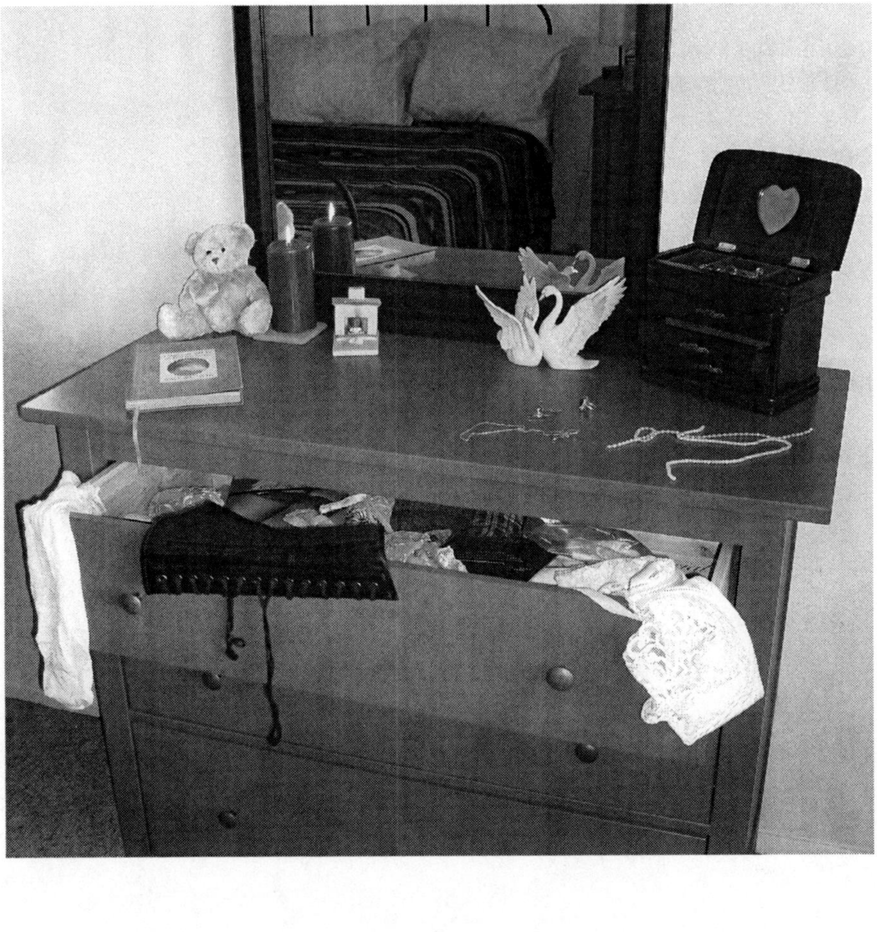

MARCH 29, 1976

Today I sat and thought...
Someday you'll grow up and move away
you'll be a man
You will be a soldier,
Or a sailor,

you'll be a husband
you'll be a father

but for today
and only for a little while

you are my precious child

and for always,
just as today

you are my son.

JESSICA

(our treasure)

good night my precious little one
there is richness painted
upon your sleeping face
that even the largest sapphire
or chests of silver
could not steal from you

James and Zavier

Harry Potter and the Incredible Hulk
woke me today
beaming beautiful boys
exploding joys
from my sleepy hollow
I rise to follow
their magical ploy
and enjoy

JC

so small
so helpless
clinging to your daddy
for today
tomorrow doesn't matter
yes little one
enjoy that sanctuary
while it lasts

shining grin
mischievous eyes
playing tag with me
how can I not smile back
despite knowing
what you have yet to learn

eyes then turning in shyness
cherub face
into daddy's strong safe chest
then quickly turning back
giggling peek-a-boo

but if you knew
what's in store for you
how long would that smile last?

the heartaches heartbreaks
responsibilities
all too quickly
this world will have your square peg
fitting into its round hole
just like your daddy.

so small
so helpless
get used to them little one
for these you will be
all your life
the smile will remain
in some form
though never again
as it is today

A CRYSTAL ROSE

(For Crystal)

When she was little
and not in the middle
 Crystal thought it nice
when asked her advice
that they two should be four; and, furthermore,
She asked and she wished for
a new sister.
But what makes her happiest
regarding her new status
Is where they now had her
on the family ladder –
sitting now in the middle row
sits a precious crystal rose.

THE GENERATION GAP

(for Douglas)

I speak to an Eighties child
about "a disposition of benevolence"
the mystic Spinoza's peace
I paint him pictures of
"the foundation of peace"
sit-ins, strikes, and civil rights.
I spin him tales of gallant knights
Sirs Gandhi, Kennedy, and King
and a land called Camelot
In Sixties naiveté, I preach of
Hope and peace
against a growing thunder.

Pointing a finger skyward
He glares out of his bedroom window
screaming "Liar!"
Breath held, I follow his gaze.
Together, we hear the sounds of
death in practice
(His Nineties reality),
as hawk shadows, Angels of Blue
again dive bomb our roof top
displaying "Top Gun" talents.

Turning quickly on my heels,
I begin a mantra walk
and breathe a prayer
for his dear sake.

JAMES

his words, breathe fire on the paper
and pour forth from strummed guitar strings
my son, the awakened dreamer,
brings modernisity to that romantic reptile
lost between science and mythology
until now

his lyrics show sad realization
that the only real dragons
are those which darken men's hearts
and he knows for sure now
that he must slay

SHY

As the Arizona Sun
peeks above Orion's fading belt
it shines upon gossamer wings
And there, she shyly remains
Until the brightest star warms her fragile frame.
It is then that she becomes strong and brave
And here the goddess' beauty is revealed
by the way she now behaves.

She dances, thinking she is alone,
Among lemon centered white petals
She makes, though she is not aware,
Smiles spread throughout the garden
So happy are they to see
The pleasant show
As she dances with the daisies
As she makes tired hearts glow.

The Holder of My Soul

Through your mom-mom's eyes the stars are alive.
Trees have spirit, and families have ties
Every new day is a brand new birth
Of the stars, trees, moon and the earth

Through your mom-mom's eyes living seeds are planted.
Funny how life seems to be taken for granted
However, I enveloped what I had
And simple things still make me glad
I try not to make a single thing sad
I taught you the wonder of stars and flowers
Made you laugh when I danced outside in rain showers
I taught you to roll down hills and lie down in the tall soft grass
Those memories will stay as long as life lasts

We'd catch butterflies that lit up our faces
I taught you to be a woman with so many graces
I always said courage is fear plus action
That our view of the world controls our reactions
Do you still see the world through mom-mom' eyes?
To see the tree's spirits, and keep family ties?
I am no saint, of that all are sure, but I am one of a kind

And Jessie
you will be the one where my spirit abides.

A PATCHWORK QUILT OF MEMORIES

(Douglas, James, and Mary)

Over there
Are the pastel blues, yellows, greens and pinks of baby powder
And cozy rocking chair feedings.
The soft textures of petal skin and downy hair,
Embroidered by the pattern of my soul.

Over here
Are the primary reds, blues and yellows of discovery.
When your minds were like flash cards
Demanding the answers to everything they saw/heard/touched.

This cool aqua marine
Represents summer revelries at the pool,
Where we were known well
For our bountiful knapsack of goodies, towels and spare change,
Freely shared with summer orphans.

See these patches? These are the wild patterned neons
Of the ambivalent and vibrant teenage years.
The music, friends, language
Each of you presented with pugnacity for our quilt,
Which I sewed firmly in place with family binding.

And here,
At the unexpected cropping of our family tree,
Is the black velvet of loss, depression, and fear
Irrevocably sewn with a locking chain stitch.
By the time I sadly sewed this,
My family quilt was done.

Sadly, this patch,
Was the last seen,
But always first remembered;

No wonder each of you turned away from me
To find your own colors in the world.

Now I stand,
a solitary, lonely oak,
Securing roots ever deeper in the warm soil of memories.
Arms branching out to the promising sunshine
And the loving dew kiss of each new day.
Foreseeing your return to spread your quilts in my shade;
New families lounging, reading, napping.
Children growing with laughter like birdsong,
With eyes like patchwork quilts.
With eyes like your father's and mine.

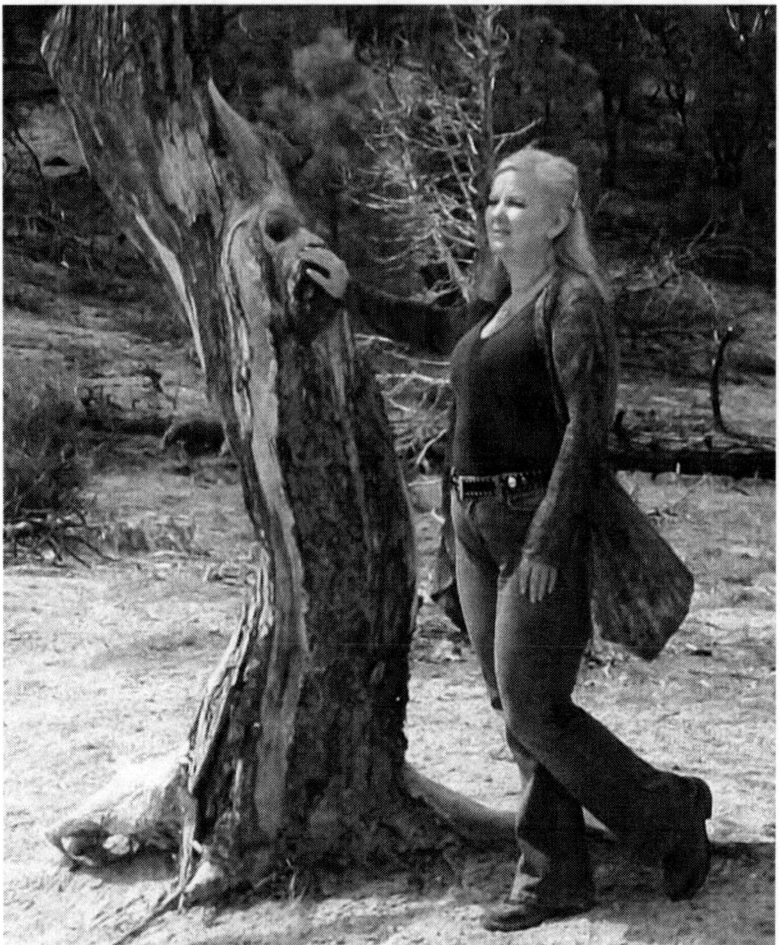

GROWTH AND SORROW

Family has always come first
But now is all you have
And tension mounts
An impassable silent
Bridge.

Your sacrifice
Their advance.

Only grace and God know
Your truths
Remembered and
Untold.

Like a candle light
Flicker.

ABUSE

love,
displayed in a glass case under the rainbow lights.

perfection standardized to meet the needs of an uncharted heart.
unknown to someone so unsure.
never loved and plenty heartbroken.

pressed to the smooth glass, shiny hope flat against something so untouchable.
a sparkle in deep-set blue eyes; batted lashes and the inspiration of the unattainable.

never before noticed
downplayed version of the window-shopping dream.
a dream set aside for future reference.
cast away for lack of understanding with no regards to the feel of regret.
left in plain sight to hinder the heart.

set aside for...
thrown on the line to be..

held on to ?
let down ?
let go of ?
pushed away ?
ripped away ?
THROWN AWAY!
moon eyes attracted to the glass.
butterfly kisses and unspoken unconditional love.

under the rainbow lights, perfection is shattered.

surrounded in the smallest shards of broken glass and
Technicolor reflections.
pieces of the soul streaking down carmine cheeks; hopeless
and alone again.

tarnished; gold flecks left on wet skin like freckles from
yesterday.
a reminder of things lost so pure.
memories of tiny arms and gentle touch.
one kiss left unrefined.

the butterfly is gone;
with life scattered in pieces at the bleeding soles of worn feet.

BROKEN

I feel sometimes
like I have truly lost my way.
Sometimes it's hard to make it
through the day

When I have the chance to sit and think
I stare ahead and never stop to blink
My heart is loudly crying out for you
My soul is crying out for a love
so pure and true.

I don't know how I've stayed so strong
I guess I am waiting for the day
When all of my pain will go away

It's been so hard without you by my side
Losing you took away so much of my joy and pride
You are a part of me
A piece of my soul
And until you find me again
There is no chance for me to be whole.

I am so sorry that I let you go
And hope one day that you will know
That all I ever wanted was the best for you
Even though its torn my world in two

The only reason I am still alive
Is the hope that you'll be by my side
I want you to know wherever you are
That even if the distance is far
You are always in my heart and soul.

I wandered Sedona where your father walks
And on that day left this in his and God's control
One day He will send you back to me
One day my heart will again be free

My love for you will never end
When you come back, my heart will mend
Just know, as I am sure you do
A mother's love is forever
Even if we are not together.

SURVIVAL

Not enough love
and too many bitter jokes
set to lighten the sad, tragic atmosphere...

Finally just be keep sane
I rushed out
of my world into some
Kinder Darkness.

Now, I dismiss love that is personal,
an emotion of luxury,
of uncomplicated lives.

Heedless of the human spirit.

OUTSIDE HER GARDEN GATE

The old leaning pine outside her desert garden gate
Senses her soul's indecision,
The final approach to a turning point;
The closing of a life.

The residue of unmet expectations,
Rotting fences of desires and needs,
Rusted entanglements of too little truth
and far too many lies,
The contradictions, the compromises--
This is the chaotic landscape
Which endlessly fills her mind;

And she wonders
How much should one endure
Before finally letting go?

How she envies the pine its pure simplicity!
Quietly drinking in the sun,
Serenely greening its leaf gown,
Taking in
Only what the wind and rain allow,
Without complaint
Never beyond the limits of its thrust

A virtue of trees,

Of every living thing

Except HER

Stuck at the surface of time and space,
Barely aware of who and why she is even here,
She finds that nothing is ever enough
Like children hurling rocks skyward
And watching them fall to the ground

Her restlessness, it seems, is sewn
In the deepest fabric of her thought:
She was designed, condemned
To always push

Beyond her conscious bounds--
To yearn for what she should not,
And bear the knowledge
Of a line to real love
that can never be crossed;
And then suddenly it becomes clear,

She realizes,
What a part of her knew all along--
Why she could not be angry
Except toward herself for being human,
Being flawed--

Hope and love--and all their illusions--
Though always short of completion
Are the only ways any one has
To transcend their imperfections
To make sense of what does not--
So she struggles to sleep
In her make believe peace.

LONELY SOJOURNER

Journeying down an old, familiar road,
One where vulnerability is forever present
once the walls get taken down.
Terrified of exposing her soul
with vulnerability always comes pain.
Many say "I won't ever hurt you"
yet in the end, intentional or not, it happens.

Most don't bother to look beyond
the outer packaging to
the delicate soul within
and those that do,
often get discouraged
since the walls surrounding her soul
are virtually impenetrable.

To even get a chance at making it
beyond this carefully guarded treasure,
an interest beyond the usual
observation of most must be shown.
A shoulder to lean on as she deals
with the emotional fragileness
left behind after the walls have fallen
must be given to prevent them
from being built back up again.

The scariest part of the journey down this road
is the thought of traveling down it alone once again.
Many times has she started down this road
with someone only to have them abandon her.
Left alone to fend for herself she contemplates
which fork to travel down.
Unfortunately, there is only one fork in the road
upon which you may travel unaccompanied
and that is the one she takes time and time again.

She holds hope in her heart
that one day she will find her soul mate
and together they will travel the many
different paths in this road with
happiness as their companion.

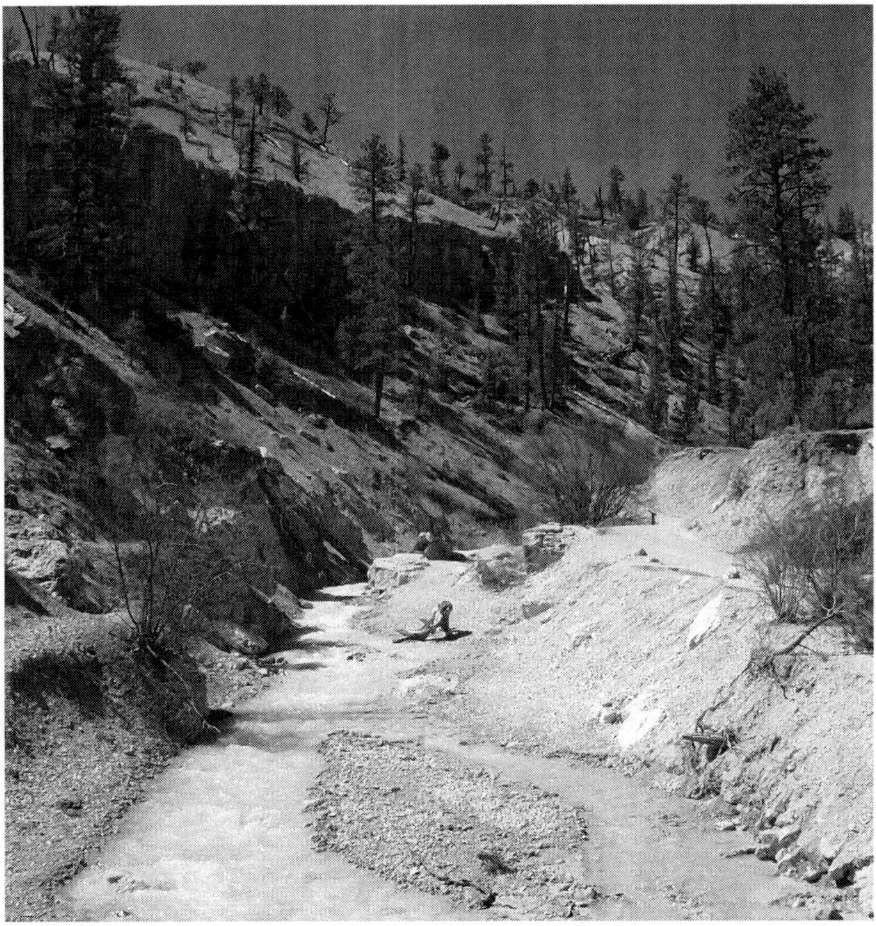

LOVE LIKE LIFE

Love, like life, is a sparkling flower,
Flowing with colors from the rainbow
Shinning with the rays of a summer sun,
But someday even the most nurtured flower
must wither away.

IMPORTANCE

Gently, a finger caresses
Finds solace in
Special touches and
Intelligent eyes of blue grey
Fixated together *we*
Are the burning
Sparkling eyes of god

On clear Arizona nights
About us revolves the
Rest of those things
We share and love
But which I don't quite
Care to know as much about

As I do
You

Winter's Promised Sleep

Once, she felt cocooned in the arms of strength
In the heart of love
In the comfort of support

Once she believed in undying love
The golden threads of friendship
The forgiveness of a God

Now the autumn moon smiles sadly
Upon a lonely figure
Who gazes up at Orion's belt.

While falling leaves swirl in the frosty air
Dancing across a heart grown cold
Disillusioned by too much of life's grief

In that emptiness she weeps
For lost love
Lost faith
Longing for winter's promised sleep

TRUTH ALWAYS WEARS A DISGUISE

In the darkness where my natural side thrives
You can hear a thud each time that one arrives
Hiding in the shadows like past forgotten lives
In the dusty corridors of the forbidden Poet's Archives
To go there with a weak heart would be most unwise
For in this hole of pain, the truth wears a disguise

THE BREAKDOWN

Body
weak and degraded
by probing hands, roaming
to find ill.

Mind
slowly disintegrating into dust
tattered by yes or no questions
answered by maybe.

Heartbroken, repaired, broken
by lovers and friends who
were pretending to be
lovers and friends.

Soul
bruised all over
from years of abuse, still
there waiting to
be healed.

Spirit
intact and hopeful and
healthier than
I, but weakening
quickly

I AM DAMNED

What will it feel like
one week after this recent surgery,
the utter absence of my real breasts
now adorned with unfeeling nipples
screaming silence
after all the frantic months
of undoing my blouse?

I will see the surgeon
at least once more,
tomorrow morning,
and he will tell me
"the incision is healing well,
how nicely it curves to my armpit,
then I will hear him telling me
as he snips away yet more stitches
it's not the most
cosmetic
scar he's seen
but very good considering.

I will quickly do up my blouse.
Ugly is sudden.
(No it is not, it creeped up on me.)
I bet he will ask if I have "emotional needs"
laugh
I had those weeks before the first surgery
and screamed them before this one
and felt them go unanswered, unheard
so.. those feelings have long since fled,
snapping the skinny ligature
binding me to the leavings of
my gone,
bountiful, feeling, gentle breasts.

Back home maybe I will try to plant
more beauty
in our garden Tom began for me

When the breasts were first cut away?
But more than likely
I will end up watching spiders
wrap and suck their prey
in every outside corner.
I want to tear the webs,
snip the silken coffins,
give the prey
that blundered in
their unexpected freedom.

Later, I will stand before the mirror
undo my blouse again,
It will be the thousandth time
I've performed this act

But tonight I am sick
I am sick
Sick to the very core of my soul
like my first view after the Mastectomy surgery,
the giant wad of gauze
parting slowly from
the fresh, red,
impossible line
illogically filled with something unfeeling
against my ribs,
the sacred site of a
razed and holy place,
to which I must concede.
In my innocence,
in my shock

I place my palm
on what is healing
tell my lost breasts
I'm sorry.
Telling "my man" I love you.
Telling my dreams
you are now a lost prayer.
I cannot resurrect again.
I am damned.

THE ARIZONA RIM

The circle of cancer
Spins around and around
Like an old antique
Mystical merry-go-round
Some horses dance up
And others dance down
To the tunes
of the Carousel's sound.

Some tunes are so sad
They tear me apart
But mostly they're happy
And a joy to my heart

Like the song of the winds
On the Arizona rim
As they dance with the trees
And the ripples of the brook
As they play with the breeze
Or the splash of the waves
As they jump on a Pensacola beach
And the laughter of a child
As she runs up to me

While I watched and listened
A a wise loving man appeared
And sat down at my side
I asked: "Would you please
join me on this ride?"

We caught the gold ring
And waltzed round and round
To the beautiful tunes
Of the Carousel's sound

Some loved ones got tired
And got off the ride
I wanted to get off
And lie down at their side
But instead I stayed on
And got back on my horse
And danced to the tunes
Of the Carousel's sound

Like the song of the winds
On the Arizona rim
As they dance with the trees
And the ripples of the brook
As they play with the breeze
Or the splash of the waves
As they jump on a Pensacola beach
And the laughter of a child
As she runs up to me

Like the song of the winds
As they danced with the trees
And the ripples of the brook
As they played with the breeze
And the splash of the waves
As they jumped on the beach
And the laughter of a child
As she runs up to me

CAMERON

Ember red glowed over the gorge
between plum-black horizon
and brooding lead thunderhead.

We stood transfixed
in wonder and awe
as rose-petal pink
sank
into a languid turquoise sea.

Until every wandering cloud
succumbed to Night's
tender veil

Would I remember
during storms to come?

How could I not
Each storm is a reminder
of Natures Order
Her wrath and her beauty

And of a power greater than us.

SOUL MATE

On a night both ethereal and gothic,
I walked an open field with
An obscure, silent companion.
an entity at once beguiling and melancholy.
It was she who had transformed the earth
In the folds of her gossamer gown,
Veiled it in the heavy curtain of her shroud.

She performed, for me alone,
A ballet with the wind
As he carried her in graceful lifts.
She pirouetted for the wail
Of a bassoon soloist
In wisps of clouds, she reveled
In the pure joy of her dance
And in the song of hope
Emitted by the resonating woodwind.

The treetops,
Where earlier she had laid her cheek and wept,
Were still heavy with those ancient tears.
Moved, now, by her performance
And the sorrow from the distant strains,
They trembled, shedding borrowed droplets
At her beauty and her grief.

Reluctantly, I left her there.
For in her, I had found a soul mate;
An answer to my confusion.
Nature and I, for one brief span,
At last were one
And I no longer felt alone.

US

When joy is
Drained
And all
Is vain,
Without grudge,
I will
Give myself
Back
To that selfless
Source
From which we came,
And become
More
Of what
We mortals mostly are;

It has no want of room
And will not judge,
In its deep, dark womb,
I will rejoin
The immortal memories
Of our ancestral past;

Do not despair
Or find me wrong,
Or doubt
Our bond,
My love,
For I will be
As near
As always was--

Yes,
If one of us
Still
Can see the stars,
As the poets have said,
We others,
Surely,
Will never be lost.

Table For One

a silent whisper:
"come here"
but
there's a table set for one.

My Life

I'm walking down the empty path
my head down and shoulders stooped
tears drip off my face
I am miserable
I have no life,
I'm not me.

I hear a noise
I slowly bring my head up
and gaze my eyes upon you
my tears dry up like the desert under the sun
my head up and standing tall
YOU have cured me
I am myself again.

I do have a life
a life with YOU!
If only in my heart.

PRELUDE TO A KISS.

my skin is silken sweet and siphoning you
intriguing and ivory with most intricate desire
I am praying rosary beads urgent, hollow
sweet hail marys, cursing, hexing my soul
which worships Your savior touch
and love, even in the most crimson blaze
my grayest hues of ash will crave the god in you
this kiss is a prelude;

AWESOME!

The lightning and the candle
Red tailed hawks flying in the sun
The strength, the warmth, the beauty
That's you, all rolled into one

The power of the lightning
Is awesome to behold
It lifted me right out of myself
We both felt the connection as you took hold

Now, my pen is in my left hand
The candle to my right
You are the lightning through the window
Illuminating my night

I turn my back unto the east
My heart now faces west
I'm drinking in Orion's power
To undertake this quest
What shall it be, I wonder?
What may soon come about
When I leap into the future
And leave behind my doubts?

What will occur tomorrow?
Or the day after that?
Will it be joy or sorrow?
What will happen after that?

It matters not, I'll take it
This is my life to live
To be close to you and love you
To give all that I can give.

The hold that you have over me
Is awesome to behold
It still lifts me right out of myself
Your connection forever holds.

ALL MY LOVE

In my "virgin" days
When this world was wild
And my aspirations
Fever hot,
Defiant of compass,
Disdainful of maps,
I scorned even the wind,
And brazenly hurled myself
Into the vortex
Of my youthful visions
With heartfelt trust,
Or so I thought…
But then such is youth...

What a painful view
Taunts me now:
An unyielding ocean
Pounding its chest,
Where once my hallowed ship
Had gently sailed;

I have salvaged
A clump of sadness,
While under my feet
Lie broken shells--
Remnants of what was,
Or might have been;

Denied the horizon,
Held to account
By a searing unforgiving sun,
Lost like driftwood
Of this desolate shore,
I retreat like a snail
Into the calcified
Memories of myself;

Reluctantly, I confess,
An impetuous flame
Still burns my cheeks,
Whenever my thoughts
Plummet backwards
To that singular day,
When he called me to him
and made my body burn with life,
And then that invisible lavender letter
ghost like arrived;
With words I first had hoped were true
And now pray were not

Words almost cryptic,
Yet deftly revealing,
Flickering with hope,
Infested with doubt--
I devoured them all,
Like a starving child;

Yes, I read it over and over,
Until I sobbed,
And cursed aloud,
Seeking certainty
Where none could be found;
I heard the sound,
Of those many lies,
Falsely witnessed
My fears reshaped
Into prudent sighs,
Convinced myself:

All love was death,
Salvation, the sky.
For far too many years now
My fight to live has proven tough
I am afraid to leave and miss you all so much
But I am afraid, this time,
my body may have had enough.

In pagan wisdom I now release my fear
And with it all my pain too
Know that you are and were my life
As are my children AND my friends
And my spirit will always live on in you.

So should the shadow of death prevail
Still I will stand by each of you
A protective spirit to guide you from above
So that you will feel every breath you take
Filled with my eternal love

Filled with my undying love…

SEASONED LOVE

You're in my dreams at night
And in my thoughts each day
My step is a little lighter
As I go along my way.

Are there special rules for love
That comes in middle years?
Or is it still acceptable to feel
Excitement mixed with fears?

My skin is scarred
and has started to wrinkle
Which you seem not to see,
And your rugged, older body looks
Wonderful to me!

All those years and heartaches
Are worth it now, it's true
For the love that I've been
Waiting for is . . . You.

HIS SMILE

(Tom)

His smile
So childlike and inviting
Is like a yellow lemon
Sun
That melts
The frozen mountain
Shadows of my
Soul.

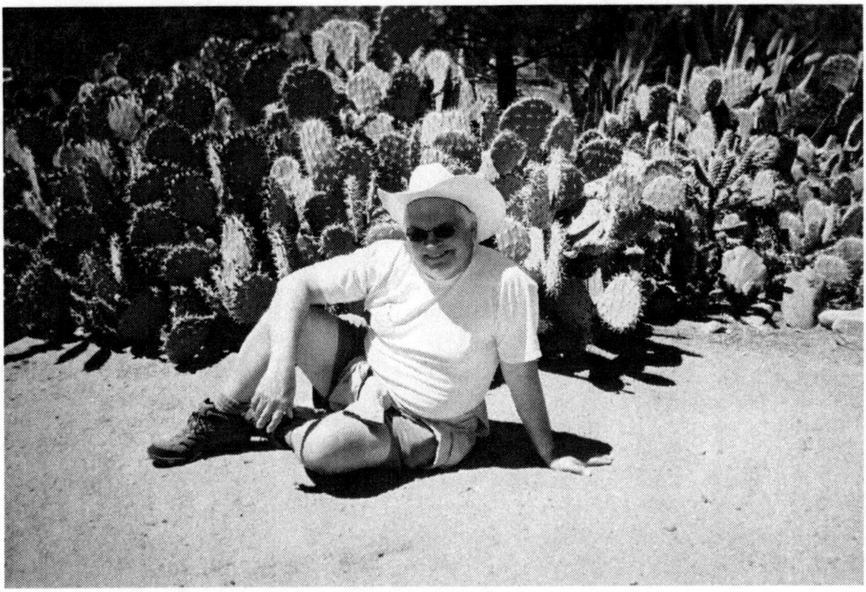

WITHOUT HIM

I was with him yesterday, but not today.
Now, suddenly I find it hard to go on this way.
I sit and wish I were still holding him tight.
I sit and wish I was with him tonight.
I wish there was an easy way out,
'Cause with him I finally learned what love is all about.
I close my eyes and feel his touch.
I never knew I could love anyone so much!

THINKING OF YOU!

A stream of tears runs down my face
as I helplessly search for your love again
Only to feel the pain that I have within,
to view the memories we had back then

To know that you're with someone new,
showing her the love you once showed to me,
the feelings that were supposed to last,
the togetherness that was meant to be

To think of you with her next to you
reminds me of the past day
when you held me in your arms
and told me, "here is where, forever, you will stay"

My heart still aches from the moment,
the very last time I felt your touch
I didn't know it was the end,
I didn't know love could end so fast, after having so much

THE MEMORY

with the moonlight slipping through the window,
I cry,
Remembering how moonlight hit your face
when next to you I would lie,
watching you sleep.
Now I am waiting for a miracle during the night,
praying you will come back to me soon,
I try to think of other things,
but the memory of you overtakes me in every way.
I imagine everything I love,
your smile, your voice, your eyes, your laugh.
I wake up suddenly realizing
it was just a sweet dream;
I am once again reliving the memory of you.

AUTUMNAL LOVE

Each calloused palm
has stayed the course
and traveled the contour
of softened flesh.
With ease he pleases
in the depths of familiarity
and brands his autumn lover
like the heat
from a fresh passion.
The soul he sings from
is ancient and wise
and has bid goodbye to a youth
careless and ignorant.
There is no fluid
to douse the fire
but the nectar
from autumn's
sweet, dark, vase.
A space of consecrated power
and splendid memories,
where he dwells
longing to sustain
the thrusts
of his youth.

TELL ME MORE

Tell me more about the willfulness you despise
While I get lost in the implications of your eyes
And breathe the scent of your manhood in.
There is none other who thrills me to this quick
Ordering the animal within me to thrash and kick
And fill my mind with sin.
It's hard to comprehend your intentions at times
Do you smirk corruptively, criticizing my rhymes
while ensuring my compliance to your lustful demands.
You lead me casually, gently down this path of pain
Honoring and desecrating the ground where we have lain
And I enter willingly into this evil pact.
The animals within us begin to fume
As you shove and stretch to make yourself room
While I am given no choice but to accommodate the ache.
"I want more," you insist as our heats combine
As our limbs, our sex, our lusts entwine
And I fall from more than grace while I thrash and quake.
Surrendered and sudden, the heat is gone
As the will I've lost turns your passions on
And your pleasure with my submission fills me with new pride.
The sharp pressure of your hunger pulsates still
And my tense throat moans as you continue to take your fill
And within my soul's womb, germinate your dark seed.
And it's hard not to pant
As your will over powers me
And it's hard not to shake
As your rough form pounds me.
And my cries grow stronger
As you bind and slap me
But my body finally softens
As you use it and trap me.

And I am left merely gasping where I lay
Wishing that you could…we could…through the day.
But morning creeps in and I moan aloud
As you abandon me… to this lonely shroud.

Sunset on the Lawn

It was some ancient injury
That never seemed to heal
The reason for his misery
He never did reveal

I loved him in my silence
Like a stranger looking on
while he kept me at a distance
Like a sunset on the lawn.

THE BUTTERFLY

Tonight, as if performing a ballet,
the trees play in the evening breeze,
A few of them are starting to turn color
A rare site in this AZ desert.

Sitting on my patio
i seek to assuage
the loneliness in my heart
with a scented candle, and chamomile tea;
fighting my surroundings
with pagan love and lore
as soft lingering clouds billow
against a diamond encrusted night sky.

i love this promise of winters cool
yet mourn the future chilly barrenness
it portends

A lone butterfly passes by,
orange and black,
wandering far from the flowers
in its curiosity.

i track its flight
which helps to empty
the sad river
flooding my heart.

Landing on my knee,
it sits, beating its gossamer wings
in time with my heart beat

i still myself
reluctant to give up its company,
letting my tea grow cold
as the butterfly teases my bare skin.

The strong western breeze
through the night trees
is the only thing moving
other than its wings.

In a whisper,
it remembers another errand
and flits off,
reminding me that there is
pure timeless beauty
that I've forgotten,
and the waters of sadness
evaporate
in the faux summer night.

VISIONS

rain softly falls
as I sit here and write
I close my eyes and
I'm greeted by visions
visions of you
your laugh
your smile
your face
your eyes
I remember the way you walk
the beat as each
of your feet
hit the carpet
the way your body moved
so ruggedly with each step
I remember you in tee shirts
your baggy shorts and flip flops
and how much tenderness that picture still brings me.
I remember you standing in front of me
forbidding me to pass
until I told you what was wrong
and comforting me when I did.
I'm hanging on to these memories
I'm reaching out
till you come home

HE MADE ME FEEL

Hands moving
Caressing
Down, down
Lips kissing
Skin, flesh
Soft and smooth
Silken
Dreams forming
Naked bodies press
Tease, taunt
Ease, haunt
Down, down
Kissing lips
Down, down
Giving in
To screams
To cries
To passions
Created by
Teasing touches
Teasing kisses
Teasing hands
Spreading thighs
Opening up
To his gift
A powerful feeling
Surging through
The entire body
Focus, focus
Focus on one point
One feeling
And know
The most important thing
Isn't how he makes me feel
But that it is him
Who made me feel

FIRST ORGASM

We rise up slowly,
As if one person.
Together we breathe,
We moan,
We shudder.
Our naked bodies intertwined,
As if an impossible puzzle.
Our minds connected electrically,
Like that of two networked computers.
We communicate without a word.
We gasp for breath.
Our bond growing stronger,
More electrically charged.

I scream as the incredible charge runs through my body.
The orgasm only a god can give.
I moan like a goddess.
Our hearts race,
As if in the Olympics.
We slow,
Hearts still racing,
Breath still pacing.
I whisper "I love you."

I WILL NOT DESERT YOU

(a promise to a new love)

Know this, my love,
I will never desert you.
I will be there when all have gone away,
When finally you have nothing more to say,
And there is no apparent reason ever for me to stay.
When all the fears of a lifetime have crowded in on you
And every particle of your past has lost all meaning,
When you cannot lift your head
or hold back the tears,
And you can no longer bear
the terror of your own ruminations,
When all your triumphs are as dust
that cannot hold you aloft,

And even the others whom you have helped
and loved have no time for you,
I will be there
To bring you what joy and courage I can,
To remind you of all the beauty and wonder
you are,
To heal you with all the love I have,
To carry you, if need be, wherever you must go,
Only because you are my love and my life
And I will never desert you.

COME!

within the shadows I whisper
      come to me
from the shadows behind the sun
      come!

I breathe and he flies
I sigh and he comes

Expectations in his eyes I cry
      Please!
quivering I fall to my knees
      please!

and I try so hard to please
and he does come
and he does come

SHADOWS OF PURE GOLD

You became my sun,
providing my warmth and life
which my yellowed greenery so desperately needed.

Your gold shadows
cast upon my trees and flowers,
opening my heart to another view
One that held only thoughts of you.

So stay high in the sky,
let your rays whisper never-ending promises,
while I open up all my petals to you.
And let you in where no one else
Has ever been.

TOMORROW

love the end of each day
watching the sun slip slowly
from sight as the Night Queen
Dark West Rising
arrives in her silver splendor.
I love the calm following the hurried pace
of the daylight hours when we do stuff..
Night wraps us in a soft velvety blue
that gentles our souls and soothes ourselves.
The end of the day is our reward
for jobs well done. Closure comes.
We settle down by the fire in Winter
or out on the porch in Summer.
There is a peace at eventide
that hungering hearts require.
It's the balm that readies us
for whatever tomorrow brings.

Empty Spaces

I'm not sure
just exactly what to do.
Actually,
I've never been so very confused.
Because for all my life,
I've been searching
for this one simple thing,
and now that I've got it,
it's leaving me.

I guess I looked
in all the wrong places
behind corners,
and in all the empty spaces.
When the one simple truth
was that all I needed was you
to fill
those empty spaces.

My life will never be quite complete
if you're not with me.
Because when winter comes
and fall leaves
your memories will be all I see.

And when my final moments have begun
I'll wish I would have known
That I looked,
in all the wrong places
behind corners
and in all the empty spaces.
When the one simple truth
was that all I needed was you
to fill
those empty spaces.

You fill my empty spaces.

ACCEPTANCE

Your gaze burns hot,
unrelenting;
blistering my soul as if lost...
lost in need...
lost in a lake of flame...

Yet;
you find me.

Time
and time again...
You find me.

Knowing;
exactly where I am...
where I need to be
Knowing my state of mind...
my unfocused focus
seeing only You;
knowing only You...
existing
only for YOU.

It was You
who told me of the Zen saying...
"One breath,
one lifetime...
its all the same to eternity."

This is how I feel;
kneeling
waiting
breathless...
for Your touch...
for Your acceptance of my offering...
of myself
in entirety.

I am that breath;
that lifetime...
held in the timelessness of Your gaze.

I await
sweetly poised;
balanced beyond belief...

I can
only be,
yours.

AWKWARD SILENCE

Hope found its native tongue
In a single gentle touch
When no words wandered
Between us
And love is only something
We created with it
In that awkward silence
Between fear and hope
In a lull in the conversation
Where we imagined ourselves safe
From reproach as well as praise

WONDERFILLED

(for Tom)

I often sit at just the right distance
watching you
Watch the world
And I listen to you talk about what you see out there

And then I wonder what you
could possibly see in me
That makes you return year after year.

Each time making me long even more
For you to stay
As love and need grow.

Amazing
How in such a brief span of time
You bridged the gap between
The heavens and my damaged soul.
And spanned the distance between
Reality and fantasy.

With you, I learned to be a little girl
And a whole woman
 all rolled into one.

Your canvas bag of magic
Must have played quite the trick
For you to bring out the best in me
And see me the way you do.

How do I see you, you may wonder?
Do you remember the gifts of kaleidoscopes
You gave me over the years?
My favorite toys of childhood ?

...

That is how I see you always
I see you through a kaleidoscope
Ablaze with beauty
color
and form
Wonder-filled and alive.

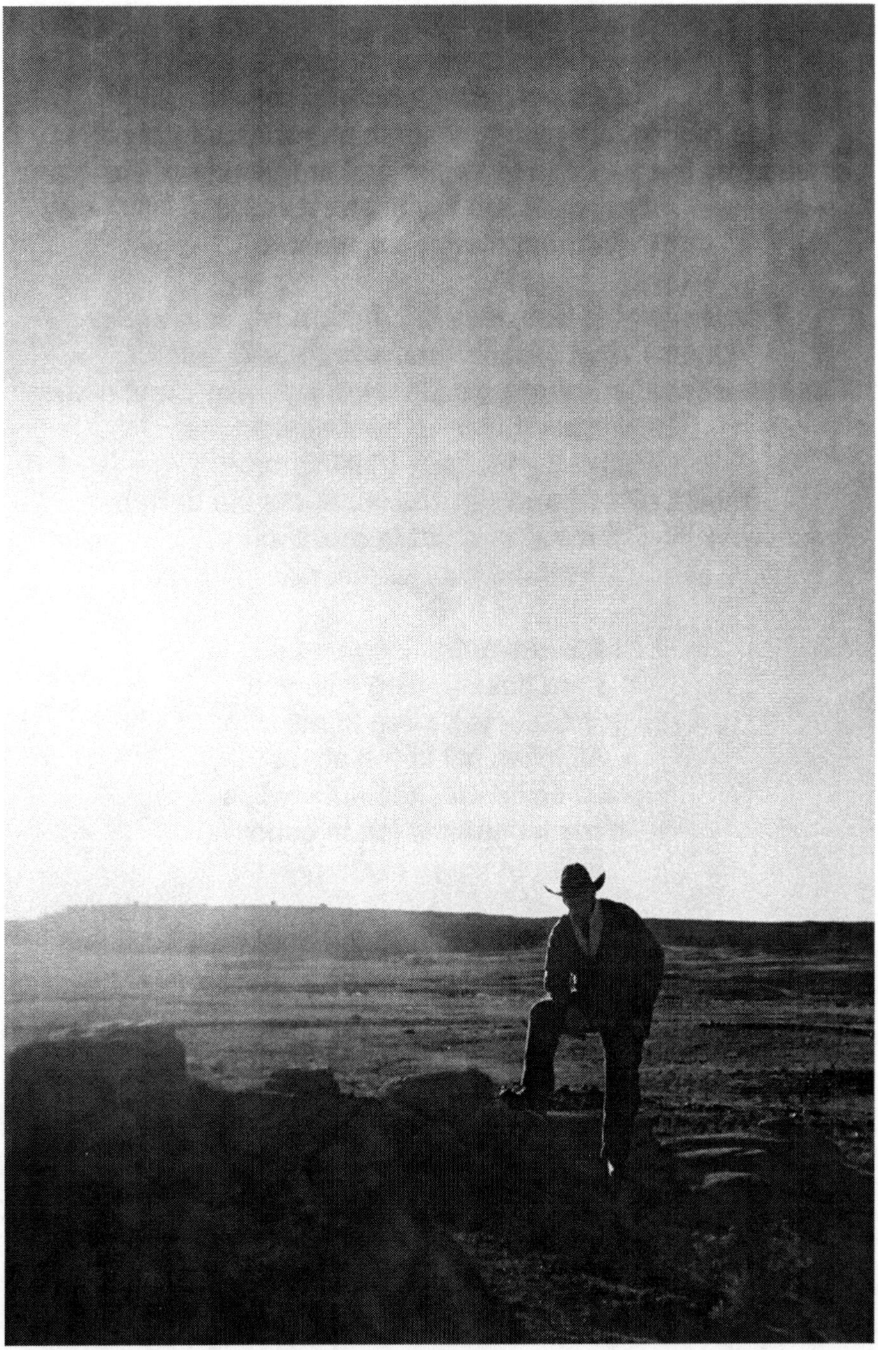

NEVER AGAIN

I never want to open my eyes again
If it's not your gaze I will see.
Let me go blind if I ever have to miss your blue gray eyes
Send away the sun and the stars and the beauty of the world
If my eyes are left to see a world
Without that pale sapphire.

I never want to feel anything against my skin again
Unless what I feel is your strong, soft touch.
The softest cashmere and gentlest silk are heavy and coarse
The warmest blanket cold against me
Without your body holding mine
Banish all soft and silk and leave me the barren
If my skin is left to feel it all
Without your caresses.

I never want to laugh again
If I am not laughing with you.
Humor is barren to me
All jokes fall to the abyss
And a smile touches not my lips
If my laughter is left to echo
Without yours in chorus.

I never want to breathe again
Unless it is your fragrance I take in.
Cleanest air is suffocating
Sweet ingests of the warm breeze chokes wanting lungs
Roses are sickly sweet
Cool autumn air is nothing to this body
If these lungs are to breathe
Without you near.

NEVER TO SAY GOODBYE

When clouds shed their sorrow upon you,
I will be your sun
shining through each crystal tear,
I will shatter each
One by one
And then a perfect rainbow
Will be born from that silver mist
And when it reaches inside your heart,
You'll know you have been kissed

And if you droop and your spirit is dying
I will tend you like a rose
And our souls will be tied
By the silver chord.
I will give you clear, thirst quenching rivers,
untouched earth, and gentle showers
I will love you and hold your damaged soul,
I will tend you like a gentle flower.

When ever you need me,
I will carry you away
To a crystal covered horizon
And a magical new day
And I will wipe every tear from your eye
And never to you will my lips sing goodbye.

Never will I say goodbye…

THE WINTER OF MY LIFE

Oh that you could be with me,
see with me
in winter!
We'd silently walk the pine scented woods
of Zion
to find the sheltered pond.
There, lichen-covered granite juts
into the ice-paned hollow
as the frosted, swirled opaque design
veils worlds of mystery beyond.

Oh that you could walk with me,
fly with me
in winter!
We'd ride the northern winds and soar
above the snow-soft earth;
brittle blue with feathers dipped
in clouds from the horizon
and tumble softly back to the gentle promise
of re-birth.

Oh that you would turn with me
burn with me,
in winter!
To melt as snowflakes on the tongues
of flaming golden oak;
and so to join the smoldered fire
of coals and burning fervor,
and rise, unfurl and dance as one
in wisps of curling smoke.

Oh, that you could be with me,
love with me
in the winter of our lives.

NATURES SHADOW.

In the shadows of
this foreboding storm,
thundering, echoing
lighting darkened sky
i ponder the truth of a chrysalis- beyond an enchanted dream

Suddenly my life is full of wonder for a transforming arty scheme
A "Free bird" amidst a rainbow canvas, a work divine
Intoxicating breath of heaven, on sweet well water wine

Delicately woven intricacy of nature's luminous parfait
Even as the wonder of a waning summer
brings an elegant bouquet
It's easy to dance with "Heavenly Wings"
Letting-go of the old for new 'exciting' things

Caught-up in the moment, the beauty of His word is true
The "Goddess of second chances" creates all things new
Now, like the butterfly, the old is left for dead
Enraptured by living scenes of beauty and wise words said

Liberated to limitless heights, free to soar and roam
With every negative there is a positive; now I rest at home
Humankind , symbolic of a butterfly, "here today and gone tomorrow"
We need truth and thankful day says,
while surrendering ourselves
to the Natural ways....

FINAL JOURNEY

The Western Sun hangs from crescent hooks
Over Cassiopeia's throne.
Below, cast in silhouetted form,
A lonely wood sprite bathes in its gentle light
And cries out to the Universe for release

In tender motions the Queen of Heaven
Dispatches Pegasus
To sooth the sprite's burning mind
With the winds of his own wings.
Then, with gentle nudges,
He urges her upon his back

Flying freely she looks down and sees the shadows
Of a long used life
And the remnants of a worn, tired body;
So battered and abused.
Looking forward, she sees her beloved Orion,
Who waits for her with outstretched arms.

Her journey, at last, is over.

EPILOGUE

Of Swans, and Love, and Carillons

"Through Autumn's golden curls we used to kick our way. You always loved this time of year…" *(Moody Blues)*

In the years prior to her fourteenth birthday, she could not recall a great deal of joy, tenderness, or love. Oh, she did find those things, from time to time, in the faces of her uncle, her godmother and her mentor; the mayor of her home town in upstate New York. However, the times she had with them were far too short, so she learned to survive in a climate of anger and abuse by keeping the world at bay. After she turned fourteen, however, she met the first man who would change so much of her life.

The young man was seventeen when they began dating in the spring of that year, shortly before the girl turned fifteen. In the early fall of that same year, he arrived at her house on a Saturday morning and told her he was taking her on a picnic. He would not, however, disclose their destination. She cuddled up beside him as he drove the big, yellow, Ford truck to "a special place", and enjoyed the aroma of fried chicken that wafted up from the basket. His mother had packed the lunch for them, and it smelled wonderful.

They entered the town limits of Lyndonville and drove through it without blinking; as to do so would have meant missing the entire town. Just as they started to exit the town limits, the young man turned off onto a dead end road. About one half mile down the road, he stopped and parked in front of a large wrought iron fence and gate. The gate was opened wide.

About one quarter of a mile inside those gates was a large,

tranquil pond on which beautiful, white swans glided in peaceful majesty. This was the place where they were to picnic, a place called "Smith's Pond". The leaves had already begun to turn russet, gold, red, orange and yellow, and the grass, which surrounded the pond, was as thick as a shag carpet. They removed their shoes to walk in the grass amid the few leaves that had already fallen, to wade in the cold pond, and to feed the swans the bread the boy had brought with him.

"Happy?" he asked. The girl, who was not prone to showing emotions, was over awed with a joy that was beyond expression. The place was right out of a fairy tale. Somehow, this boy had stepped into her dreams, ripped a place of peace right out of them, and set it down in the middle of her reality. On that day, the boy taught her to trust him and to love him.

"For a man shall leave his mother; a woman will leave her home. They shall travel on to where the two shall be as one..." (*John Denver*)

Those were the words, as sung by Peter, Paul & Mary, that a young bride of eighteen heard as she walked up the aisle to become united with a handsome twenty years old groom. For the next twenty-three years, those words continued to ring true as this young couple grew closer together, built a family, celebrated the joys of success, and found solutions to life's upheavals while working together as one viable unit. Everything they did was performed as one unit, and they always believed that, as long as they were together, nothing could ever defeat them. Military separation did not defeat them, for their spirits were always united across the miles. Illness did not defeat them, as the woman suffered miscarriages, Multiple Sclerosis, increasing bouts of Epilepsy, throat cancer and breast cancer. The diagnosis of their youngest son's brain damage did not defeat them as they took their love and surrounded him in its cocoon. The brutality of the outside world did not defeat them even after an "animal" broke into their home and brought the woman's past rushing ferociously into their present. Addiction did not defeat them as they fought the disease together through love and commitment. Together, they moved through life like a well-oiled machine. Together, they built their world.

"Our house is a very, very, very fine house…" *(Crosby, Stills, and Nash)*

On May 28, 1993, the woman and her husband finally bought their first home in what they thought was a well-developed, safe neighborhood. They had been dreaming of this day for twenty years. Shortly after his retirement, they began the search for the sanctuary where they hoped to finish raising their children, and then enjoy their autumn and winter years together.

Initially, the home they chose met every expectation. The neighborhood was equally populated with young married couples, families in the middle of raising their children (teens), and retired couples. The neighbors on either side of them were friendly and maintained their homes and lawns exceptionally well.

However, change was in the air and, considering the ever - growing military and retirement community which became the controlling populace of the county in which they resided, inevitable. Unfortunately, most of the changes were not positive ones. Recently purchased homes were no longer being maintained, which greatly reduced property values. The lack of state taxes often did not permit adequate maintenance of streets or sidewalks, and the roads, unless main thoroughfares were in a chronic state of disrepair. Litter laws were not upheld and the results could be seen in trash strewn everywhere. Although these "changes" made the previously serene and green subdivision now appear depressed, sad and worn, they were not the changes that had the most negative effect on the neighborhood. That effect could be directly attributed to gangs that had infiltrated almost every neighborhood in the city, but had selected the suburbs as the prime territory to terrorize.

Drive by shootings became a weekly occurrence. Families or couples could no longer take evening walks together for fear or violence or theft. Even the ability to sit on their front porches and chat as neighbors was taken from them. The Sheriff's Department, although doing their best to apprehend gang members, proved ineffective. They became prisoners in their own home. Their house was no longer a sanctuary or a retreat; it was a fortress. A fortress which was now being invaded by one of their own; their special needs child had become a member of "The Pensacola Syndicate". Therefore, they made the decision to leave a dream that had turned into a nightmare in an attempt to save their child and their own form of sanity. However, before they got to act on that decision, the choice was taken from them. The man was diagnosed with arteriosclerosis disease and congestive heart failure.

Rocky I've never had to die before,,, (Austin Roberts)
Chameleon-like his skin changed color from pink, to ash-gray, to the color of starched hospital linen. Earlier, the external tissues had begun to take on water that the pump could no longer remove, over flowing the banks of the heart with toxins. Suddenly, a vacuum sucked the oxygen from the room, and the death squeeze began again.

Placing his body on a thin, metal table in a room maintained at meat cutter's temperatures, they plugged it into electric monitors, painfully piercing it with three needles connected to two plastic and one glass bottle, as they talked and laughed; impervious to the death stalk.

Chants to the Goddess went out and worry stones worked in hands grown older as she stood, once again, at the gate of widowhood; too young, still too young. She longed to rip the pump that tortured her love from its cage and strangle it with her own bare hands. She longed to hold the body she loved, tenderly, and caress it until it hurt no more, but gently slept.

Watching gauges and listening to blips on a screen, warnings of the future that lay beyond that day, wanting only to climb onto that butcher's board and absorb the pain and cold from the body she had loved for twenty plus years, she stroked the boiled clam skin, now cooling too rapidly.

Courage held, waned, and held again as the infant day began amid instruments of steel, winter white walls, and medicinal smells. While better living through chemistry brought sleep and respite from excruciating pain and pressure.

Sitting alone at a distance beside a window filtering light into a room of shadows, she read poetry, prayed, and planned, then watched in gratitude and love as deep set green eyes in a placid face opened wide and smiled at her. The heart she loved still beat like a metronome, and time was still theirs to share.

On November 6, 1997, a doctor informed this couple that the man had only one year or less to live, and their world came crashing in around them.

"If I had to live without you, what kind of life would that be...?" (*Mariah Carey*)

On September 2, 1998, the union of this man and woman was dissolved as The Universe called the groom home and left the bride a widow. Although a fairly resilient woman, the widow had always been able to rely upon someone else to assist in the decision making process, lean on when she grew tired, complain to when she was hurt, or curl up beside when she needed closeness. Suddenly she was faced with a void of unimagined proportions; financial problems to solve, legal battles to fight, and a family still to raise while she herself battled physical health problems, fears for her own future, and a depression filled loneliness. She had always been someone's daughter, then someone's wife, and then someone's mother. She was used to being useful or used for and by others. Now she was simply herself, and the matriarch of a family that was turning to her for all of the answers.

Aware of the grieving process from having counseled others touched by the hand of death, many of them AIDS and Hospice patients and families, she was spiritually and mentally prepared for the problems that she faced. Still, her first response was to keep the world at bay by putting up a strong front so that her children would not be afraid, and extended family members would not deem her weak. During the course of each day, she would laugh and talk with the neighbors, her friends, her children, but always at evening time she would cry. The result was despondency and the inability to heal. She felt empty and loveless.

"Spread your broken wings and learn to fly" (The Beatles)

Two years elapsed and this woman became consumed with suicidal ideation. The feelings that she had bottled up so tightly within her were destroying her very soul. Finally, with the help of a vvery loving friends, who forced her to accept the feelings she held within, she began to speak of the anger that raged inside her heart and soul. She was angry with her husband for leaving her behind. She was angry for the way he had treated her in their life together. She was angry over the fact that she did not know what real love was. She was angry over the loss of her home to foreclosure after the VA failed to respond quickly enough on her deceased husband's disability payments. She was angry with the Universe. She was angry at the thought of being in debt, becoming ill, or becoming a burden to others. Most importantly, she was angry with herself for allowing herself to be so abused throughout her life. However, with love and support, she worked her way out of what could have become a debilitating depression and began to build her life as a single person with a remarkable support system

"I am everything I am, because you loved me…."Diane Warren

She decided to continue on with the plan she and her husband first had when they learned he did not have long to live, which was to remain in Arizona with her brother, buy a house together with him and his partner, and begin to pick up the pieces. When she, her brother, his partner, and two of her children moved into the new house, one room was totally set aside where she could find solace and fill it with memories of family, lost love, and hope. A room that she would use as her writer's garret and complete the book she had promised to see published. This became the sanctuary in which she would retreat to find peace and understanding when the world grew too much for her. Always, outside the door, she knew her brother, her brother-in-law, her children, and her grandchildren waited to give her the courage to face another day.

She insured that her children were able to stand alone without her and, with everyone's backing, decided to enroll in college after a 25-year absence from formal learning. With each class completed, she learned to allow her family to help her celebrate her accomplishments, where once she had only celebrated for everyone *but* herself. With each accomplishment, she began to heal and to grow.

"Where are the prophets? Where are the visionaries? Where are the poets?" (Marillion)

Finally, she started to write again and began working on the dream she had always held, and which the love of her life had also held for her; she began writing a book. Again, she learned to share her successes in this area with her immediate family and friends, and felt the healing and exhilaration she received from their love and support. She had learned that one times zero makes one; one hell of a successful, competent woman who had known great love and still had the love of so many others surrounding her. She had learned to love and nurture herself.

"I know you're out there somewhere" *(Moody Blues)*

That young bride of eighteen, who gave birth to three wonderful children, worked, loved, and was widowed at the age of forty-two, was I. Although I had been aware for more than one year that my husband was terminal, I never thought I would have to live my life without him; nor did I consider it possible. However, once I learned that in order to stand alone as one I had to first love myself and then accept the love and support of others, I found that I could rebuild my life. I miss my husband, but I believe that he is watching from some other plain and is very proud at how I have chosen to move forward with my life. I also feel that, in so doing, I am showing my own children and grandchildren what it takes to pick up the pieces and rebuild your dreams when "life happens while you are busy making other plans".

"Give me something to believe in..." *(Poison)*

And then, while I was busy making those other plans, the fates stepped in once again and brought a special man into my life; one with wisdom, unassuming leadership, and a heart large enough to hold the world. He came into my life just at the moment I had decided I would **never** form another relationship and that I would spend my remaining days alone. He came at a time when I had shored up the walls to my heart, my soul, and my mind with titanium steel, vowing no one would ever gain entrance to me. Funny how we are delivered into the hands of fate...

Neither of us intended for anything to really come from our meeting but perhaps friendship and maybe even mutual satisfaction. In my case, however, doors were opened to emotions I had either never been allowed to have or else prevented myself from feeling. Love was always something I gave but never allowed myself to receive. Now, everything involving my relationship with this very special man became things I wanted to do, things I wanted to give, things filled with love. At the age of 49 (the autumn of my life), I finally experienced physical, emotional, and mental feelings I had never experienced in my life and I found myself falling in love again and in many ways for the very first time. I also found I was in love as well. Falling in love is generally considered to be a physical dynamic... and perhaps that is true. But, **being** in love is the glue that holds two people together in some way; permanently. Being in love means that you are growing spiritually and mentally while allowing the one you love to grow as well. This is the greatest form of love that I believe a man and a woman, or two men, or two women can ever share. It is this love I now know for the first time as he lets me grow... and I hopefully am helping him do the same.

I Want To Be In Love (Melissa Ethridge)
Thanks to the wonderful 50th birthday party given to me by my children and my oldest son's gift of flying Tom down to me, we were finally able to meet in true time together; but prior to that, it was his heart, his mind, and his soul, that brought all of me to life again... or maybe, as I have come to truly believe, for the very first time. I also hope, that my children, my friends, and even Doug (wherever his spirit now resides) rejoice with me and for me. For in my autumn years, I have found love one more time. I have never known the happiness or joy that I found over the course of the last four years. I have never laughed so much or felt so young. For all of this, I am eternally grateful.

Not many women can be blessed in such a way... to know the souls of two men and to be so much in love with one in the here and now. I wish this blessing for all of you, men and women alike. I wish you each this joy and, yes, this sorrow too. You cannot know one without the other. I am happy to now have known both...

Blessed be...